BEAT THE SLOTS

ACKNOWLEDGMENT
To my dear friend Nancy Snow, whose skillful manuscript editing helped make this a better book.

ABOUT THE AUTHOR
Marten Jensen, the "Doctor of Gambling," is one of the foremost authorities of gambling in the world. An expert on all the casino games, Jensen is also the author of six books on beating the casinos, all published by Cardoza Publishing.

Great Cardoza Publishing Books by Marten Jensen
Secrets of the New Casino Games
Secrets of Winning Roulette
Video Poker & Slots for the Winner
Beat the Slots
Beat Multiple Deck Blackjack
Beat the Craps Table

BEAT THE SLOTS

Marten Jensen

CARDOZA PUBLISHING

Cardoza Publishing is the foremost gaming and gambling publisher in the world with a library of almost 100 up-to-date and easy-to-read books and strategies. These authoritative works are written by the top experts in their fields and with more than 6,500,000 books in print, represent the best-selling and most popular gaming books anywhere.

FIRST EDITION

Copyright© 2002 by Marten Jensen
-All Rights Reserved-

Library of Congress Catalog Card No: 2002101911
ISBN:1-58042-063-X

Visit our new web site (www.cardozapub.com) or write us for a full list of Cardoza books, advanced, and computer strategies.

CARDOZA PUBLISHING

PO Box 1500 Cooper Station, New York, NY 10276
Phone (718)743-5229 • Fax (718)743-8284
email: cardozapub@aol.com
www.cardozapub.com

TABLE OF CONTENTS

1. INTRODUCTION   7

2. BEATING THE SLOTS   9
Why You Need to Read this Book!
Important Decisions
A Little History

3. SLOT MACHINE BASICS   17
Slot Machine Families
Cabinet Styles
The Manufacturers

4. SLOT MACHINE ELEMENTS   25
The Paytable
Reels, Symbols, and Paylines
Special Symbols
Play Buttons
Displays

5. MONEY MATTERS   37
Denominations
Coins, Bills, and Credits
Tokens
Cash Tickets
Cashout and Handpay

6. PLAYING ADVICE   45
The Playing Environment
Tipping
Slot Clubs
10 Important Tips for Slot Players

7. OPTIMIZING THE PAYBACK   57
Microprocessor and RNG
Machine Payback
The Odds of Hitting a Jackpot
Finding the Loosest Slots

Payback Cycles
Testing Your Machine

8. SPINNING REEL SLOTS 69
Coin Multipliers
Multi-Line Games
Option-Buy Games
Banking Games
Video Versions of Reel Spinners

9. BEATING THE SPINNING REELS 75
Study the Glass
Coin Multipliers
Multi-Line and Option-Buy Machines

10. VIDEO SLOT MACHINES 83
Bonus Games
Banking Games
Multi-Game Machines

11. BEATING THE VIDEO SLOTS 87
Bonus Games
Banking Games
Multi-Game Machines

12. PROGRESSIVE SLOTS 111
Stand-Alone Progressives
Local Progressives
Wide Area Progressive Slots

13. BEATING THE PROGRESSIVES 115
Strategy for Stand-Alone and Local Progressives
Strategy for Wide Area Progressive Slots

14. ODDS AND ENDS 123
12 Slot Machine Misconceptions
Slot Tournaments
Buying Antique Slot Machines
About the IRS

15. GLOSSARY 135

INTRODUCTION

BEAT THE SLOTS? Is that really possible? You bet it is, and this book will show you how to do it!

It will teach you how to maximize your chances of winning on every different kind of slot machine in the casinos. It will show you how to find the best machines to play and how to play them to win. It will even tell you how to find and play games in which you have a better than even chance of winning the money.

Should you play the reel spinners or the video machines, or should you stick with the progressives? This book will fully describe the features of every type of game and how to play it in the most effective manner. We will also show you how to find the loosest slots and how to test a machine to see if it is hot.

Do you know the difference between a multiplier, a line game, an option-buy game, and a banking game? If you don't, you will certainly go through your gambling stake very quickly. We will advise you on the best way to play every one of those games, and which ones are the money makers.

Let's now see how to make money at slots!

BEATING THE SLOTS

Just by thumbing through this book you can see that it is brimming with useful information about every kind of slot machine. When you decide to read the details more carefully, you will learn how to extend your bankroll, and you will even learn how to legitimately overcome the casino's mathematical advantage on some games. These are things that couldn't be done on the old machines—at least not without cheating.

Fifty years ago, a few slot machines were tucked away in the corners of the casinos, or in back hallways. Today, electronic gaming devices (an industry term that includes slots, video poker, video keno, etc.) are everywhere and account for almost three-quarters of the total revenues in all American casinos. Considering the huge popularity of slot machines, it is somewhat curious that there are still relatively few good books on the subject. We hope this one helps to fill the void.

Why You Need to Read this Book!

Not long ago, there was little point to reading a book on slots—if you could even find one. Most of the machines were similar: they had three reels, a coin slot, a coin tray at the bottom, and an actuating lever at the right side. You dropped in a coin and pulled down the lever. The reels spun, and if you were lucky, you won a few coins.

Over the past ten to fifteen years, however, slot machine technology has undergone a major revolution. Many machines today have become a form of computer game, which has little resemblance to the old mechanical contraptions of twenty or more years ago. Yet, other than pushing a button instead of pulling a lever, most slot players have not changed their playing style.

Typically, they enter the casino with a few hundred dollars in their pockets, plop down at any unoccupied machine, and spin the reels. When they eventually run out of gambling money, they go see a show or just go home. If they do get lucky and win a jackpot, they keep on playing until they have given all their winnings back to the casino. They never expected to come out ahead, anyway. That is the sum total of their casino experience.

Modern slot s are no longer the mindless one-armed bandits of yesteryear. Now they are all sophisticated computer-controlled devices, although the ones with actual mechanical spinning reels do try to hide the fact that they are fully controlled by modern technology.

So how does this affect you? It means that if you are not completely familiar with the game you are playing, and if you are not playing the best way possible, you will likely lose your money at a faster rate than the designed-in payback would indicate. So how do you avoid falling into this trap? That's simple! Just read this book.

IMPORTANT DECISIONS

Most people think that, unlike video poker players, slot players don't have to make any decisions—they just drop in coins and hit the SPIN button. WRONG!!! Slot players have plenty of decisions to make, and if they make wrong decisions, or arbitrary ones, they will rarely come out ahead. So what are these important decisions?

The first, and most important one, is the selection of the right machine. But aren't they all basically the same? Absolutely not! There is such a variety of slot machines in the casinos, made by numerous competing manufacturers, that some of them are bound to be better than others. The trick is to know how to tell the good from the bad. This book will give you the inside scoop.

Once a suitable game is selected, your second decision is to determine how many coins or credits to wager on each spin. Today, there is no such animal as a single-coin slot machine. All modern machines take multiple coins, and the misguided advice to always bet the maximum can cause serious damage to your wallet. You need to know which games are best played with a minimum wager and which always require the maximum. Do it wrong and you will reduce your chances of winning. We will tell you which is which.

But things get even more complicated. How do you play a game designed to accept as many as 90 credits at a time? Do you really want to play a nickel machine and invest as much as $4.50 on a single spin? We tell you how to tackle that and similar situations.

Slot machine manufacturers are always trying to invent new ways to encourage people to keep on paying and playing. In their enthusiasm, they have devised a class of machines we call banking games, in which points or some type of assets are accumulated and finally paid out as a big bonus. Knowledgeable players have discovered that these games often reach a point when they are profitable to play.

You may find it hard to believe that some casino slot machines are actually beatable. Believe it! We will show you how to locate these slots and how to win the bonus. As you read this book, you will learn details on many related topics, such as advice on finding the loosest machines, the advantages of joining slot clubs, and the safest ways to deal with the IRS. We also tell you about slot tournaments, slot machine misconceptions, and which states permit you to own an antique slot machine.

All the ringing bells, flashing lights, and clattering coins tend to mesmerize the majority of slot players. They sit at a machine and spin the reels as fast as they can, hoping they will win one of those big jackpots that they perceive are being won all around them. They believe that if they keep feeding the machine and keep those reels spinning, sooner or later they will also be big winners. And then they wonder why they keep on losing.

Once you have read and absorbed this book, you will look at those players and chuckle. They think slot machines are mindless games requiring no particular strategy, other than pure luck, and that some people are just luckier than others. But you will know better. You will know that by learning about the games and by using a methodical approach, you are much more likely to come out ahead than those poor, unenlightened amateurs.

A LITTLE HISTORY

The spinning reel slot machine was invented over 100 years ago by August Fey, a German machinist who had immigrated to San Francisco. His invention was called the Liberty Bell, which was a three-reel device in a metal box that contained symbols such as bells, stars, and horseshoes. The top prize was paid when three bells appeared in the window, and it was popularly called a Bell machine. That name stuck for a long time, being generically applied to any slot machine.

Fey's machines soon became very popular, and in 1907, an enterprising fellow in Chicago by the name of Herbert Mills copied Fey's mechanism and started manufacturing slot machines on a large-scale basis. Mills modified Fey's design, however, in that his machine had 20 symbols per reel instead of 10. He also widened the window so the player could now see three rows of symbols, but only the row under the centerline paid anything.

Being able to see winning symbols that just missed the payline, encouraged people to keep playing with the thought that they might hit it big on the next pull. This teaser window design soon became a standard feature.

Before long, Mills' slot machines were being distributed throughout the country and were installed mostly in saloons and pool halls. In 1912, Nevada legalized slot machines as a form of vending machine, so long as they did not pay out cash awards. This started a period during which slot machines paid winners with chewing gum and other products. The reels carried pictures of various fruits that represented the different flavors of gum, and some of these symbols are still in use today.

The Mills Novelty Company was very successful and by the late 1920s had more than 1000 employees. During the prohibition period, slot machines evolved into full-fledged gambling devices and rows of them could be found in every speakeasy. By that time, slot machine manufacturing had become a big business, drawing in other competitors, but Mills remained the leader.

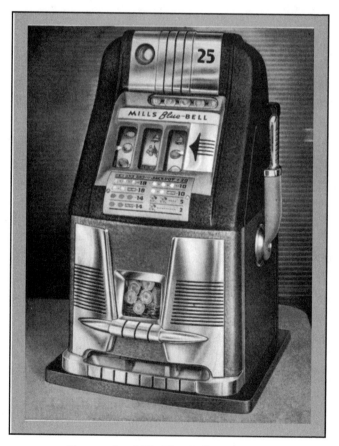

The popular Mills Blue Bell, circa 1949

By the early 1930s, most slot machine installations were controlled by the mob. When Mayor Fiorello LaGuardia ran the slots out of New York City, the mob took them to New Orleans by invitation of Governor Huey Long, who made millions in kickbacks. Machines controlled by the mob had such a poor payback (typically about 50%) that they became known as "one-armed bandits."

Meanwhile, after Nevada legalized gambling in 1931, the first legal casinos installed slot machines for the purpose of distracting and entertaining wives and girlfriends, while the serious gamblers played at the gaming tables. By the time the Flamingo Hotel opened in 1947, many casinos began to view slots as a profit center and improved the payouts to attract more business. This enticed some of the serious gamblers to the slots and began a long-term escalation in the popularity of slot machines in gambling casinos.

All the early slot machines were purely mechanical devices, the internal mechanism consisting of wheels, gears, levers, springs, and cams. In 1931, the Jennings Company developed the first electromechanical slot machine with motor-driven reels. It was not very successful because, at that time, many gamblers were wary of such new-fangled technology.

Further improvements were minimal until the 1960s when Bally Manufacturing Company (now named Bally Gaming Systems), a major supplier of pinball machines, entered the market with newly-designed electromechanical slots. Soon Bally was introducing machines with multiple coin acceptors and motor-driven coin hoppers that were capable of making much larger and faster payouts. These machines were so successful that, by the 1970s, Bally controlled 90% of the slot market.

In 1975, the development of the first all-electronic video slot machine by the Fortune Coin Company constituted a major departure from the traditional electromechanical machine. In 1978, the Sircoma Company, later renamed International Game Technology (IGT), bought out Fortune Coin, and the product line was soon expanded to include four-reel video slot machines. Although slot machines with video screens were not that much different than their mechanical cousins, they ultimately led to the introduction of video blackjack machines, quickly followed by video poker machines.

IGT had bet its future on the video concept. The versatility and proliferation of video poker and video slot machines resulted in IGT supplanting Bally as the market leader. Today, IGT is the industry powerhouse, although Bally is working hard to make a comeback.

It is interesting to note that over the years the original concept of the slot machine has not significantly changed. Many of today's slots still have three vertical reels with various symbols and an operating arm at the right side (although the arm is rapidly disappearing). Modern machines use credits instead of coins, accept bills of all denominations, and may even have more than three reels, while the purely-electronic games simulate spinning reels on video screens—but the basic form remains the same.

SLOT MACHINE BASICS

For a long time, a slot machine consisted of three side-by-side *reels* that displayed pictures of bells, bars, sevens, and various fruits such as cherries, lemons, and plums. The action was entirely mechanical and, after inserting a coin, the reels were set in motion by pulling down a long handle at the right side. The machine paid off by dropping coins into a tray when certain *symbols* lined up in the window behind the horizontal *payline*.

Those old mechanical slot machines are now considered to be antiques. Although modern slot machines still use the basic principle of spinning reels with symbols on them, they have become very sophisticated computer-controlled devices. Instead of pulling a handle (which is still an option on some machines), most players activate the reels by pushing a button.

Today, almost all slots take multiple coins and have built-in paper currency validators that accept any denomination from $1 to $100. In some of the newest machines, there are as many as six simulated spinning reels displayed on a video screen, using a large variety of symbols.

SLOT MACHINE FAMILIES

Since the 1980s, when the first video and computer-controlled slot machines appeared in casinos, the number of different types and styles of machines has virtually exploded.

To get a better understanding of the seemingly endless variety of slots on the casino floors today, we will begin by organizing them into the following three families.

1. SPINNING REEL SLOTS

These are machines with actual mechanical spinning reels, although the reels are completely computer controlled. Specific strategies for playing reel spinners are covered in a later chapter. The major kinds are as follows:

Multiplier Game
The payout is multiplied by the number of coins or credits wagered.

Multi-Line Game
Additional paylines can be activated by wagering more coins or credits.

Option-Buy Game
Additional winning symbol combinations are activated by betting the maximum number of coins or credits.

Banking Game
Points or some form of assets are accumulated in a "bank" and eventually paid out as credits.

2. VIDEO SLOTS

These are the newest generation of machines where the spinning reels are simulated on a video screen. The playing strategies for most video games are quite different than for reel spinners and are covered in a separate chapter. The major kinds are:

Bonus Game

Certain symbol combinations cause a bonus mode to appear on a secondary screen.

Banking Game

Points or some form of assets are accumulated in a "bank" and eventually paid out as credits.

Multi-Game

The player has a choice of several different games on a single machine.

3. PROGRESSIVE SLOTS

These slots have a dynamic top jackpot that grows larger by pooling a fraction of each wager as the games are played. Groups of machines are usually linked together, all contributing to the same progressive jackpot. Progressive playing strategy is significantly different than the strategies used for reel spinners or video games, and is therefore covered in its own chapter. The major kinds of progressive machines are:

Stand-Alone Progressive

A solitary progressive slot machine that is not linked to any other machine.

Local Progressive

One of a bank or carousel of similar progressive machines that are linked together within a single casino.

Wide Area Progressive Slot (WAPS)

One of a large number of similar progressive machines that are linked together over a wide geographic area such as a city or a state.

CABINET STYLES

When you look at the different slot machines in a casino, you will note that they come in a variety of cabinet configurations. To reduce the confusion, we will boil them all down to the following three basic styles:

1. Upright

This is a vertical cabinet that can easily be played while standing or sitting. It often comes with a backless stool. In the nicer casinos, the stool will have a back, but it's still not a very comfortable place to sit for a long period of time. It may or may not have a pull-arm on the right side, and the coin tray is at the bottom. The cabinet appearance can vary in that it may have a flat top or a domed top, but these are just non-functional style features. This is a popular cabinet with the casinos because it uses a minimum of floor space.

2. Slope Front

This is a low-profile cabinet, allowing the player to be comfortably seated in a normal-height chair. It has a sloped horizontal playing surface on which the buttons and the reels (or video screen) are located. The coin slot, bill acceptor, and coin tray are all grouped together at the right side of the playing surface. This cabinet style never includes a pull-arm, allowing the cabinets to be abutted next to each other. In some machines, the rear structure can be rather tall because of a top box with additional game features.

3. Table Top or Bar Top

These are the video units that are built into a bar top. Like the slant top, the coin slot, bill acceptor, and coin tray are all to the right of the video screen. The seat, of course, is a barstool.

THE MANUFACTURERS

As recently as thirty years ago, there were very few slot machine manufacturers. At that time, Bally was the big gun with 90% of the market. Today, there are more than a dozen companies competing for floor space in casinos around the world. In 2001, however, the competition weeded out two companies that had been major technical innovators. Following is a list of the most important slot machine manufacturers, including the two that were gobbled up by the big boys.

International Game Technology (IGT)

IGT's first big success was the Fortune Model 701 Draw Poker machine, which was introduced in 1979. This product started the phenomenal growth of video poker popularity. Then, in 1986, IGT originated the concept of wide-area progressive slots when they convinced a number of casinos in Nevada to install the Megabucks machines. These machines, and their offspring, were so successful that today IGT is the largest slot machine manufacturer in the world. They continue to be the leader in the wide-area progressive field with Megabucks, Quartermania, Wheel of Fortune, and Jeopardy, to name a few. IGT's most popular reel spinners include Double Diamond, Triple Diamond, Double Diamond Deluxe, Red, White & Blue, Sizzling 7s, and many others. Game King, which is their multi-game video slot, has also done quite well.

Bally Gaming Systems

Bally is the oldest of the current crop of slot manufacturers, and can be credited with a number of firsts. In the early 1960s, they successfully marketed an electromechanical machine, followed by the first multi-coin slot and the first video multi-game slot, the Game Maker. Before getting into the slot machine business, Bally was a major supplier of arcade games and pinball machines. Their hottest progressive games are the Betty Boop series. Other popular Bally games are Black & White Double Jackpot, Blazing 7s, Stars & Bars, and Wild Rose.

WMS Gaming

Another innovative company, WMS made their first big splash with Piggy Bankin', which was the first banking game to hit the casino floors. Although their clever banking concept was quickly copied by other manufacturers, WMS continued to attract attention with Boom, Filthy Rich, Reel 'Em In, and the popular Monopoly series.

Sigma Game

First licensed by the Nevada Gaming Commission in 1984, Sigma pioneered the built-in currency acceptor, which is now found in almost all slot machines. In 1990, they marketed the first slant-top slot machine, which was considered a major improvement in player comfort. Sigma is best known for its very popular series of Treasure Tunnel games.

Aristocrat Gaming

A major player in Australia since the 1950s, Aristocrat jumped into the European market in the 1960s, but didn't get licensed in Nevada until 2000. Since then, this innovative company has successfully penetrated the U.S. market with video games that have second-screen bonuses and scatter pays, such as Chicken, Jumpin' Joey, and Tropical Delight.

Anchor Gaming

Definitely not a copycat, this company created some of the more unusual games of the past few years. Anchor is noted for its Casino Bowling and Wheel of Gold, which is actually a top box that attaches to existing machines. VLC, a subsidiary of Anchor, quickly followed Bally into the multi-game market with its Winning Touch series. They also found a niche with video second-screen bonus machines such as Polly & Roger. In December 2001, Anchor became a subsidiary of IGT.

The following two companies were bought out in 2001. We are listing them because they were historically important participants in the slot machine manufacturing industry.

Silicon Gaming

Silicon Gaming was started in 1993, went public in 1996,

and shipped the first production Odyssey machines in 1997. The multi-game Odyssey series were advanced technology machines with superb graphics and excellent sound. To accomplish this, they utilized a fast hard drive, a CD-ROM drive, and a Pentium processor, which made the machines expensive to produce. Consequently, Silicon had trouble staying in the black and was ultimately bought out by IGT in 2001.

Casino Data Systems (CDS)

Another technology leader, CDS was mainly known for Bingo and Baseball. They also marketed several pure video games such as American Pride, Egyptian Gold, and Top Dog. Sadly, their failed attempt to cut into IGT's progressive market with Cool Millions ultimately led to their demise. Aristocrat Gaming acquired the company in 2001.

SLOT MACHINE ELEMENTS

To fully understand how a slot machine works, it is helpful to know the functions of its various components. Although, in times past, slot machines consisted of little more than a coin slot and an actuating handle at the right side, today they are far more complex with many buttons, displays, and symbols. In this chapter we explain the purposes and uses of the major elements found in modern machines.

THE PAYTABLE

Every spinning reel machine has the payouts for the winning symbol combinations shown on a posted paytable (also known as the *glass*). The table is usually located on a panel above the reels and, in some cases, is so extensive that a portion of it is below the reels.

It is very important to study the table carefully before starting to play. Among other things, it will tell you if the machine is a multiplier or an option-buy—very important information to know. (These machines will be described in detail in the *Spinning Reel Slots* chapter.) The paytable also provides the information you need to decide if you should play maximum coins or if you can reasonably play one coin at a time.

Some video machines also have posted paytables, but on most of them you have to press a button to bring the paytable to the screen. This button may be marked PAYTABLE or SEE PAYS. With their bonus and banking features, video paytables can be quite extensive, but it is always worthwhile to study them.

REELS, SYMBOLS, AND PAYLINES

As the name implies, spinning reel slot machines contain spinning *reels*. These are side-by-side rotating wheels with pictures of various *symbols* on the outside rims. A small section of the reels may be viewed through a window, which usually displays about three rows of symbols. Originally, the symbols were pictures of bells, bars, sevens, and various fruits such as cherries, lemons, and plums. In modern slots, there are hundreds of different symbols—just about anything the machine designers can dream up.

Across the center of the window is a horizontal line called a *payline* (see illustration). If a winning symbol combination falls directly under the payline, a payoff occurs. The position of a reel when it comes to rest is called a *stop*. A reel may stop when a symbol is under the payline or when the blank space between two symbols falls under the payline. A blank space is equivalent to a symbol, and some games actually provide a minor payout for three blank spaces. The symbols just below or just above the payline do not count, unless otherwise stated on the payout display.

In video machines, spinning reels are simulated on a

Slot window with a single payline

video screen. Some video machines mimic the popular three-reel spinners, while many others display five simulated reels and three rows of symbols. Such machines always have multiple paylines, and the blank spaces have been eliminated.

No matter if the reels are mechanical or simulated on a video screen, almost all of today's machines are under the full control of built-in microprocessors and random number generators. More on that, later.

SPECIAL SYMBOLS

Considering the proliferation of new symbols in modern slot machines, it is nothing short of amazing that many of the symbols used 50 to 100 years ago can still be found on some of the most popular machines. In any casino, a quick look around at the various paytables will show plenty of bells, 7s, and cherries, all of which are historic symbols dating back to the early days of the 20th century. Lately, however, slot manufacturers have come up with some new twists, which are described below.

Substitute (wild) Symbols

Since we can have wild cards in a poker game, then we should be able to have wild symbols in a slot machine. And, sure enough, we do. Many machines now contain symbols that substitute for any other symbol on the reels, thus they are called *substitute symbols*. These wild symbols can combine with other symbols to produce a winning combination. For example, 7, 7, Wild will give the same payout as 7, 7, 7, and Bar, Wild, Bar will result in the same payout as Bar, Bar, Bar.

Multiplier Symbols

As you are examining the payout schedules, searching for that perfect machine, you might enjoy playing one that pays double or triple for certain payline combinations. Such machines have a doubling or tripling substitute (wild) symbol that will multiply the payout for any winning combination.

Two doubling symbols on the same payline will quadruple the payout, and two tripling symbols on the same payline will multiply the payout by nine! In addition to multiplying the payout, these symbols act as wild cards in that they automatically become any other symbol to create a winning combination. Most of these are IGT machines and the most popular ones are called Double Diamond and Triple Diamond.

Machines with 5x and 10x multipliers are becoming more prevalent. These multipliers operate on the same principle as doubling symbols. For example, if two 10x symbols appear on the same payline, the amount of the payout is multiplied by 100! IGT has a couple of these called

Five Times Pay and Ten Times Pay.

Nudge Symbols

How many times have you been rankled because a pay-off symbol appeared just above or below the payline? You probably can't count the times when the reels came to rest with two bars on the payline and the third bar just one stop above or below the payline. Exasperating, isn't it?

Not missing a beat, IGT designed some machines with certain symbols that are nudged to the payline after the reels stop spinning. The best example is Double Diamond Deluxe, which is a three-reel machine with Diamond Bar *nudge* symbols. When the reels stop and a Diamond Bar appears above or below the payline, that reel will move one stop up or down, depending on which way the point of the diamond is facing. Since the diamond is superimposed over one, two, or three bars, this nudge symbol will complete a row of bars. Another example is the Balloon Bars game, where a hot air balloon will float up to the payline if it landed one stop below.

Keep in mind, however, that nudge symbols are just a psychological gimmick. You may think you are getting a second chance, but the internal microprocessor had already determined the final position of the reels before they even started spinning.

Scatter Symbols

When certain symbols appear anywhere on the screen of a video game, a payout can occur. These scatter symbols do not have to be lined up on any payline, but there usually needs to be at least three of them showing.

Spin Till Win Symbols

When this symbol appears on a payline, the reels will respin by themselves and keep respinning until they stop on a winning combination. Which winning combination you end up with is an entirely random process.

Repeat the Win

Although there is no particular symbol involved, some machines will sometimes respin the reels after a win to repeat that win. Whether or not this occurs is supposed to be randomly determined.

Any Bar (on paytable)

Many machines have single-, double-, and triple-bar symbols with separate payouts for each type. The Any Bar designation on the paytable means that, on a three-reel machine, you get a payoff for any mix of three bars, regardless of type.

Any Symbol (on paytable)

This is similar to the Any Bar designation on the paytable, except that you will win with any mix of symbols, so long as there is no blank under the payline.

PLAY BUTTONS

Nearly all of the functions of a slot machine are initiated by electrical pushbutton switches that are activated by a player. In most video games, the functions also appear on the video screen and may be activated by touching the screen. The most common buttons on reel spinners and video games are as follows:

Play buttons on a nine-payline game

BET ONE

Pressing this button will register in the machine as a one-credit bet. It is exactly the same as if you put one coin into the slot, which is an alternative. If you press the button a second time, it will register as a two-credit wager. If you press it a third time, you bet three credits, and so forth. On some machines, this button is marked BET 1 CREDIT.

PLAY 1 LINE, PLAY 3 LINES, etc.

This row of buttons is found on 5-reel video games and typically gives you a choice of 1 line, 3 lines, 5 lines, 7 lines, or 9 lines. If you don't press any button, some machines default to the maximum number of paylines.

BET 1 PER LINE, BET 2 PER LINE, etc.

After selecting the number of paylines on a video game, you have to decide how many credits per line you want to bet. The usual choice is 1 through 5, although on some games you can bet as many as 10 credits per line. This type of machine usually does not have a SPIN button, so pressing the BET PER LINE button activates the reels.

BET MAX

Pressing this button causes two actions to occur. First, it registers a maximum credit bet, whatever it might be for that machine. If it is a two-coin machine, it will register two coins; if it is a three-coin machine, it will register three coins and so forth. Second, it automatically spins the reels; you don't have to press the SPIN button. On some machines, this button is marked PLAY MAX CREDITS.

REBET

Pressing this button spins the reels, repeating the exact wager you made on the previous spin.

SPIN

After indicating the number of credits you wish to bet or after inserting one or more coins, pressing this button starts the game by causing the reels to spin. If you did not wager any coins or credits, the button does nothing. On some machines, this button is marked SPIN REELS.

A few machines still have a pull-handle at the right side. Pulling this handle does exactly the same as pressing the SPIN button; in fact, it simply activates an electrical switch that is wired in parallel with the switch under the SPIN button. In times past, when machines had only a pull-handle and no SPIN button, the average rate of play was 200 to 250 spins per hour.

Today, with almost everyone using the buttons, the average rate of play has gone up to over 400 spins per hour. You can bet that the casinos will completely phase out the pull-handles as quickly as they can.

HELP

Most video games have a HELP button that brings up a screen with information for novice players, such as the purpose of the various buttons, the configuration of the paylines, and what to do if something malfunctions.

PAYTABLE

Pressing this button on a video game brings the paytable to the screen. Often, it is several pages in length. Sometimes this button is marked SEE PAYS.

CASH OUT

Pressing this button converts any credits accumulated in the machine to coins that are noisily dumped into the metal coin tray. You would normally do this whenever you are ready to leave that machine or any time you want to convert your credits into coins. In casinos that use cash tickets, you will receive a ticket instead of coins. The ticket can be converted to currency by any cashier at that casino. This button is sometimes marked CASH/CREDIT or COLLECT.

Before pressing the button, always note how much credit you have, and then, after the coins have stopped dumping, check the credit meter again to be sure it registers zero. If it doesn't, call an attendant by pressing the CHANGE button (see below). If a large number of credits is involved, pressing the CASH OUT button may result in the appearance of an attendant who will pay you by hand.

CHANGE

Pressing this button illuminates the service light on top

of the machine, summoning the change person. Besides calling for change, you should also press the button any time something seems to go wrong with the machine. This button is often marked SERVICE.

DISPLAYS

There are several displays to help the player keep track of bets, credits, and amounts won. There may be some location and terminology variations between different types of machines, but they all perform the same basic functions.

COIN IN

This indicator shows how many coins or credits you have committed on the next spin. On some machines, it may be labeled BET or COINS PLAYED. Somewhere on most machines is a sign that states: **Pays Only on Coins Accepted.** So, before you hit the SPIN button, be sure that the machine accepted as many coins as you intended to bet.

LINES BET

This indicator shows how many paylines are currently activated, based on which PLAY LINES button you pressed.

BET PER LINE

This indicator shows how many credits you intend to wager on each payline, depending on which BET PER LINE button you pressed.

TOTAL BET

This is the total amount of your intended wager, which

is the number of activated paylines *times* the number of credits per payline.

CREDITS

This keeps track of the number of credits you have accumulated in the machine. The denomination of each credit is the same as the game denomination; that is, if you are playing a quarter machine, each credit is worth 25¢. The total number of credits goes up whenever you slide a bill into the currency acceptor. On a quarter machine, for example, a ten-dollar bill will add 40 credits. The number of credits also goes up when the machine pays off a winning combination. On the other hand, when you press the BET ONE or MAX BET button, the appropriate number of credits are deducted from the total.

WIN PAID

Whenever you win, the amount of the payout is shown by this indicator. This amount is also added to the total in the CREDITS indicator. On some machines, this display is labeled PAID or WINNER PAID.

INSERT COIN

This message is illuminated whenever the machine is idle with no bets registered. It turns off when a coin is dropped in or a credit is bet.

COIN ACCEPTED

When you drop in a coin, this message lights up to tell you that the machine is ready for a spin. Of course, the message will not illuminate if the coin is rejected and drops through to the coin tray.

MONEY MATTERS

As we all know, slot machines are driven by money—money that you risk and money that the casino hopes to keep. Not very long ago, the only money needed to activate any gaming device consisted solely of coins. Today the money takes on several different forms, including paper currency, credits, tokens, and cash tickets. Coins, in fact, are becoming one of the less important kinds of money used in modern slot machines.

DENOMINATIONS

The denomination of a slot machine is defined as the smallest amount of money needed to spin the reels. The casinos and the slot manufacturers have taken this about as far as possible, in that there are machines in all the following denominations on the casino floors: 1¢, 5¢, 10¢, 25¢, 50¢, $1, $2, $5, $10, $25, $50, $100, $500.

Coincidentally, except for $500, these are exactly the same denominations currently issued by the United States Treasury Department. Apparently, if you have an odd coin or bill in your pocket, the casinos want to be sure you have a place to spend it.

Yes, there are still penny slot machines out there. The new ones accept paper money and allow you to bet up to 250 coins, so they are quite profitable for the casinos.

The advice, however, is to not play them because they tend to be very tight.

At the other end of the spectrum are the $100 and $500 machines. If you haven't seen one of these, just step into the high-limit slot area of the classiest casinos. The majority of the machines, however, accept nickels, quarters, or dollars—quarters being the most popular in most venues.

As you search through the casino aisles looking for games in your favorite denomination, pay attention to the lights on top of the machines, known as candles or service lights. They are color-coded according to denomination, which can be a help in locating your favorite games. If you forget the following code, you can easily remind yourself just by looking at the different machines when you get to the casino.

RED	=	nickel
GREEN	=	dime
YELLOW	=	quarter
ORANGE or GOLD	=	half dollar
BLUE	=	one dollar
PURPLE	=	five dollar

When most slot machines began accepting paper money and registering credits, it was inevitable that multi-denominational machines would be the next step. And, sure enough, they have arrived. Some of the first ones offer a choice of 5¢, 10¢, or 25¢, while others offer a choice of 25¢, 50¢, or $1. All the player has to do is insert a bill and then push a button indicating the denomination choice. After that, the machine plays like any other.

COINS, BILLS, AND CREDITS

Not very long ago, almost all slot machines accepted only coins and paid out jackpots by dumping coins into the metal coin tray with a loud clatter. Then came the credit machines that converted coins to credits and paid out winnings by running up more credits on the credit meter. The only time you would hear the clatter of coins was when someone pushed a CASH OUT button.

Today, almost all machines accept bills and register the amount on the credit meter. As the casinos hoped, most players now find that playing credits keeps their hands cleaner and is generally more convenient than inserting coins into a slot. The advantage to the casinos, of course, is that by speeding up slot play, it increases the casino take.

TOKENS - THE PRESENT

In many midwestern riverboat venues, such as Illinois, Indiana, Iowa, and Missouri, the slot machines only accept casino tokens, not U.S. coins. This began in Iowa where the first gambling statute included a $200 per player loss limit.

To enforce the law, a system was set up whereby each patron was given $200 in vouchers when entering a casino. Then, every time any gaming chips or slot machine tokens were purchased, a voucher had to be presented. The slot machines accepted only the casino tokens; if they accepted U.S. coins, gamblers could easily get around the law by carrying regular coins into the casino.

The loss limit law was ultimately repealed, but the tokens are still in use because the casinos like them. They know that most customers will not leave with a few leftover tokens in their pockets. Some will cash them in, but many will just drop them in a machine on their way out. Another reason the casinos like tokens is that they have fewer assets tied up in the coin hoppers of hundreds of machines. A quarter is worth 25 cents, but the tokens cost only pennies apiece to have minted, consequently the token system improves the cash flow and other casino accounting numbers.

TOKENS - THE FUTURE

To avoid the handling problems of six different coin denominations, some casinos are testing a new token system devised by some inventive Australians. Under this system, now commonly used in Australia, all machines, regardless of denomination, will accept only special dollar-value tokens. If you play a quarter machine, for example, the token will register as four credits. Now the coin counter in the change booth only has to handle the one denomination. Whether or not this will catch on in the United States is still an open question.

CASH TICKETS

Another solution to the coin-handling problem is the use of cash tickets. When you cash out, instead of dumping a bunch of coins into the tray, the machine spits out a printed ticket. You may then bring the ticket to a cashier and convert it into real money, which is more convenient than toting around a bucket of coins.

For the casinos, the advantages are even greater. They

no longer have to employ all the people who spent much of their time filling and emptying coin hoppers and spent the rest of their time keeping records on where the coins went. The lines at cashier cages move faster because buckets of coins don't have to be counted, and there aren't any jammed coin counters holding everybody up. Oh yes, the casinos do love the tickets.

Typical cash ticket used in many casinos

The newest generation of cash ticket can be inserted into another slot machine as though it was real currency. These tickets have a printed bar code (see illustration) that the machine can read to register the appropriate number of credits. Although the tickets look as if they are easily reproducible with a copy machine, don't try it. Each one contains a unique numeric security code. Any attempt to use or cash a second ticket with the same code will set off alarms.

This completely coinless system has become prevalent in Tribal casinos, and several Las Vegas casinos are trying it out as well. When the newest casino in Las Vegas, The Palms, opened its doors in 2001, all of its slot machines had cash ticket capability. Clearly, the use of cash tickets is rapidly spreading.

If you play in a casino that uses cash tickets, handle the tickets you receive as if they were cash. Actually, you should handle them more carefully than that because they are printed on thin paper and are more fragile than greenbacks. Not only are they fragile, but they usually expire in 30 days, so be sure to cash them in before leaving the casino.

Of course, this evolution toward cashless gambling will eventually lead to the use of smart cards that will credit and debit your account as you play. Such cards are currently under development and are expected to be similar to slot club cards. As you can well imagine, these coinless and cashless systems only benefit the casinos and are especially detrimental to compulsive gamblers.

CASHOUT AND HANDPAY

At some point in your slot play, you will want to cash out your credits. You must do this by pressing the CASH OUT button. Before pressing the button, however, note how much the machine owes you. Then, after it has finished dumping coins, check the credit meter again to be sure it registers zero. If it doesn't, then either the coin mechanism jammed or the hopper ran out of coins. This is the time to call an attendant by pressing the CHANGE or SERVICE button.

When cashing out, a machine will only dispense a certain maximum number of coins because of limitations in the coin hopper capacity. Depending on the denomination of the particular game, this number may be anywhere between 500 and 1000 credits, as indicated by a sign on the cabinet. If the credit meter exceeds that number, pressing the CASH OUT button will bring an attendant instead of the expected clatter of coins. The attendant will first check the machine and then *handpay* you with paper currency.

All jackpots of $1200 or more must be hand paid by an attendant to meet the IRS requirement of submitting a W-2G form. Many smaller jackpots are also hand paid to keep from depleting the machine's coin hopper. For instance, on a nickel machine, a win of over $50 amounts to more than 1000 coins and will certainly be paid by hand. Whenever you receive a handpay jackpot, don't leave the machine without checking the credit meter for credits you may have previously accumulated. Then press the CASH OUT button to get what it owes you.

Finally, whenever you play the slots, be sure to carry some form of legitimate photo identification, such as a driver's license. For a payout of $1200 or more, the IRS requires the casino to verify your identity for the W-2G form. If you do not have a photo ID in your possession (a slot club card will not do), you'll have to jump through a number of hoops to get your money.

PLAYING ADVICE

The casinos make sure that playing a slot machine is a relatively simple procedure: You insert a coin or a bill, press a button or two to make the reels spin, and if the right symbols line up behind the payline, you win some money (or credits). If the winning symbols don't line up, you lose your investment and (the casino hopes) you try again. However, in the real world there is more to it than that, and this chapter covers those other aspects of slot play.

THE PLAYING ENVIRONMENT

When playing the various table games in a casino, the patrons soon learn that there are certain rules of etiquette and protocols that need to be learned if they are to avoid nasty stares from other players and admonitions from the dealers. To a certain extent, the same is true when playing slot machines. Although the slots are played individually, there are times when interactions do occur with other players. It may be self evident that the normal rules of etiquette and courtesy would apply, just as for any other endeavor, but some people need to be reminded what they are.

This may be because playing slot machines is different than ordinary activities, and the casino environment is different than ordinary environments. Just so that you know what is expected, we will explain the correct approach to use for some situations that may not arise in everyday life.

When you are looking for a suitable slot machine to play, do not crowd the other slot players. Slot machine play tends to be a solitary activity, so many patrons do not like a stranger looking over their shoulder while they are spinning the reels.

Before you sit down at a machine, be certain that it is not in use. Check that the person sitting one or two seats away is not playing more than one machine. Ask, if necessary. A cup on the handle, a purse or sweater on the chair, an inserted slot club card, or a burning cigarette, are all signs that someone stepped away from the machine for a moment. Yes, it is foolish to leave personal belongs at a machine to reserve it, but that's what some people do.

If you want to reserve a machine while you go to the restroom, ask an attendant and he/she will usually accommodate you by placing a RESERVED sign on the machine. If the casino is not crowded the attendant may even agree to reserve the machine while you go to dinner. However, the casino will not be happy if you reserve one machine and then go off to play another.

Although most casinos have an overabundance of security people, don't let that lull you into doing foolish things like placing your purse in the space between two machines. Always keep it on your shoulder or on your lap.

Laying down rolls of quarters is also not a good idea; keep them in your pocket or purse. Always assume that there are opportunists hanging around in every casino waiting for you to let down your guard.

Better yet, don't bring a purse when you go gambling. A fanny pack is more secure, but only if you keep it strapped securely to your body. As soon as you remove it, it is no safer than a purse. The best approach is to carry everything in your pockets.

Finally, successful players are aware that alcoholic intake dulls a person's judgment. Consequently, most of them never drink alcoholic beverages during a playing session, reserving this activity for when they are celebrating a big win or bemoaning their losses.

TIPPING

Let me say at the outset that I don't believe in tipping, unless a service has been rendered in a particularly efficient and pleasant manner. In a casino, tipping is never required. You are in total control as to when, where, and how much to tip.

Something many people are unaware of is that if you give someone a large tip for an instance of extraordinary service, your tip will be shared with the other employees in that service group on that shift. To comply with IRS regulations, all tips must be pooled and taxes withheld by the employer before the remaining money is divided among the workers. So your big tip is first taxed and then the balance is split up evenly between all the workers in that group. Sometimes, even the lowest level of supervision shares in the tip pool. This doesn't seem to bother some people, but it bothers me.

In a restaurant the tipping situation is well defined. The 15% tip has become so standardized that many patrons leave 15% whether the service was good, bad, or mediocre. In a casino, however, there are large gray areas. So much so that many people overtip when tipping isn't even indicated.

Let's start with the change lady. (I know that's not politically correct, but I've rarely seen a man doing this job). Change ladies are not normally tipped for making change. So the conventional wisdom is that if a change lady provides a special service, a tip would be appropriate. What sort of special service could she provide? I don't really know. Changing a hundred-dollar bill? But that's her job, and changing a hundred is not a particularly difficult task. This is probably becoming a moot point, now that almost all machines accept paper currency.

I've read in some books that you should tip a change lady who directs you to a "hot" machine. Granted, that *would* be a special service, but how could she know which machines are hot? And if she really knows, why aren't her friends playing them? However, if you walked away from a game, inadvertently leaving your purse behind or some credits in the machine, and the change lady chased you down, that *would* be worth a tip!

After winning a jackpot, you might tip the change lady, just because you feel generous. But then, shouldn't you also tip the person who paid you off and the security guard who accompanied this person? How about the minimum-wage person who cleaned up the coin wrappers and the ash trays around your machine? Should you tip all these people? Remember that you will probably pay taxes on your winnings. Any tips you give out will be pooled and taxed as well.

The other service provider that you encounter while playing slots is the cocktail waitress. This is a no-brainer. You normally tip her 50¢ to $1 per drink, depending on her efficiency and the complexity of the drink you order. If you are playing a dollar machine, I suggest you tip at least a dollar or you will look like a cheapskate.

SLOT CLUBS

Most people believe there is no such thing as a free lunch. If you also believe that, then you haven't spent much time in Las Vegas. Slot clubs actually give you more than a free lunch. You can get a free room, a free dinner, and maybe even a free show. Of course, to get these comps you have to play the machines. But then, that's what you are doing anyway, so you might as well cash in.

For the slot machine and video poker player, slot clubs have no down side. Slot clubs operate on the same principle as frequent flier clubs. They are designed to encourage you to gamble in their casino by rewarding serious players with various comps. This is done with a computerized player tracking system that keeps tabs on each player's activity so that the comps can be awarded in a fair and consistent manner.

The best approach is to determine which casinos you prefer, and then join their slot clubs. This is easy to do—it takes only a few moments to fill out a slot-club application. You will also have to show them some form of photo identification to verify your identity. The main purpose of the application is to record your mailing address so they can send discount coupons and information on special promotions. In most casinos you will be given some discounts or comps just for signing up.

After you have signed up, you will be issued a coded card so that the computer can track your playing habits. The more you play, the more points you rack up. These points can then be traded in for a variety of comps. Even if you don't use the card very much, the casino will notify you of slot tournaments and mail special offers to entice you to come in and play.

When you play a machine, be sure to always insert your card so that you can accumulate points. Every slot machine and almost every video poker machine has a card reader that accepts slot-club cards. Remember, however, that the card has to be from the casino in which you are playing. When you insert the card, a screen display will greet you by name and may even tell you how many points you have accrued. When you leave the machine, be sure to retrieve your card.

If you forget or lose the card, however, don't worry—you can easily get another. In fact, most casinos will honor a request for two cards so that you can play two machines at the same time. Furthermore, you and your spouse can combine your accumulated points by setting up a joint account.

If you are a regular player, the comps from most slot clubs will add 0.1 to 0.5% to the total amount of your wagers, and some will add as much as 1%. Some casinos even offer cash rebates. These comps and rebates are based on the total *action*, which is much larger than the amount you actually risk.

Let's say you start with $20 worth of quarters and spin the reels at the leisurely rate of 400 times an hour. After just two hours of play at five coins a spin, you have cycled all 80 quarters through the machine 50 times (400 spins x 2 hours x 5 coins ÷ 80 quarters = 50). Whether you came out ahead or lost the entire $20, you generated $1000 worth of action (800 spins at $1.25 a spin = $1000).

Many people do not realize how little money has to be at risk to generate those comps. Be sure to take advantage of the available comps by always using your card.

10 IMPORTANT TIPS FOR SLOT PLAYERS

TIP #1
Be sure to always insert your slot club card.
In some casinos, using your card can effectively increase the payback of the machine you are playing by as much as one percent. You haven't joined the slot club? If you've read the section on slot clubs, you will know that there is no down side.

TIP #2

Play only what your bankroll can handle.

When you arrive at a gambling resort, you should first ascertain what denomination of machine you should be playing. To help you determine this, the following table shows how much bankroll is needed for a two-, three-, or five-coin bet in each denomination, assuming eight spins per minute and a 90% payout rate:

	2 COINS	3 COINS	5 COINS
Nickel machine	$5/hour	$7/ hour	$12/ hour
Quarter machine	$24/ hour	$36/ hour	$60/ hour
Dollar machine	$96/ hour	$144/ hour	$240/ hour

Next, decide how many hours you would like to play over the course of your stay. For example, assume you start with a bankroll of $600 and would like to play an average of five hours a day for three days. That is a total of 15 playing hours. Dividing 15 hours into $600 gives a rate of $40 per hour. Thus, you should not play anything more costly than a three-coin quarter machine. Of course, in actuality, you may win more or lose more than the 90% payback would indicate, but at least you have a reasonable starting point.

TIP #3

When you insert coins, be sure you get what you pay for.

Like any equipment with mechanical components, slot machines are subject to considerable wear and tear. This is especially true of the coin mechanism. After handling hundreds of thousands of coins, the mechanism will malfunction sooner or later. Your best protection is to observe the glass and the paylines as you insert each coin to be sure the correct sections light up, showing that they are properly activated. If you hit a winning combination that doesn't pay because only two of your three coins registered, you are out of luck. If one of your coins doesn't register, be sure to wave down an attendant or press the CHANGE button and wait for someone to arrive. Don't spin the reels before the situation is rectified.

TIP #4
Play one machine at a time.
Slot managers know that some people like to play two slots simultaneously, so they always flank a loose machine with tight ones on both sides. At best, you will win from a loose machine only to lose your winnings to a tight one; at worst, you will lose to two tight machines. Two loose machines are never knowingly placed alongside each other.

TIP #5
Never play the machine right next to someone who is winning.
If the winner's slot is loose, the machines on either side will be tight. Of course, the winner's machine may just be a moderate payer that turned hot, but you don't know that for certain.

TIP #6
Stay with a hot machine.
Never leave a machine that just paid a big jackpot. By

definition, it is a hot machine that could continue to pay out very nicely. Don't abandon the machine unless it has not paid anything for six consecutive spins.

TIP #7
Observe other players who are winning.
Watch players who are winning regularly and keep an eye (and ear) out for sudden jackpot winners. For any number of reasons, these people may occasionally leave *while their machines are still hot.* If you see that happen (and your machine is cold), move over to the other machine before someone else gets there. Why would a person leave a hot machine? Many slot players think a machine turns cold after paying a big jackpot. Or maybe they have a dinner reservation or tickets for a show. If the machine is still in a hot cycle, their loss is your gain.

TIP #8
Abandon a cold machine.
Don't throw good money after bad. If, after six spins, the machine has paid out very little, abandon it. If available, move over to the slot right next to it. Tight and loose machines are often placed side by side.

TIP #9
Never leave a machine that owes you money.
Sometimes when you hit a big jackpot, an attendant has to make the payoff, or sometimes during a payoff, the machine's hopper runs out of coins. *Stay with the machine no matter how long it takes the attendant to arrive.* Occasionally a machine malfunctions and you can't redeem your credits, or the bill acceptor gets hung and eats your Franklin without giving you credits. *Stay with*

the machine no matter how long it takes for a mechanic to arrive. If you leave the machine, you will have trouble claiming what is rightfully yours.

TIP #10

Don't forget to press the CASH OUT button.

Most machines accumulate credits as you play, and you must press the CASH OUT button to convert the credits into coins. Even if you have just won a hand-paid jackpot, before leaving the machine, press the CASH OUT button and be sure the credit meter reads zero. If it doesn't, call an attendant because the machine may need a hopper fill, or the coin mechanism may be jammed. If you are distracted when you leave your machine and forget to cash out, someone else will get to enjoy your winnings.

And finally, remember the cardinal rule of slot play: QUIT WHILE YOU ARE AHEAD, BUT NEVER QUIT WHILE YOU ARE WINNING!

OPTIMIZING THE PAYBACK

With the exception of banking games (covered in the *Beating the Video Slots* chapter), playing slot machines is usually a losing proposition. All machines are intended to be profitable for the casino, and each one has a designed-in payback percentage. In many cases the payback is fairly good, but careless playing techniques can make it a lot worse. Knowledge of the characteristics of machine payback helps players to avoid mistakes that result in a poorer than optimum return.

MICROPROCESSOR AND RNG

All slot machines today are *microprocessor* controlled. Microprocessor is the term used for the dedicated computer board inside the machine, which is the electronic brain of the game. It is very similar to the computer you may have at home, except that it serves the single purpose of controlling all the functions of the slot machine including the movement of the mechanical reels. In video slots, the screen is similar to the monitor on a home computer, except that it usually has touch-screen capability.

In most gaming jurisdictions, new models and styles of slot machines have to be approved by the local gaming commission before they can be installed. The main concern of the gaming regulators is that the random number generator (RNG) in each machine is operating properly.

The RNG is one of the chips on the internal computer board. It generates thousands of random numbers a second, and each random number sequence defines a specific set of reel symbols. The instant a player presses the MAX BET or SPIN button, the next set of randomly-generated numbers is selected.

The program uses this set of numbers to define the symbol combination that will appear under the payline on the reels or on the video screen. A fraction of a second after the player hits the button, the program has already determined the final position of the reels—before the reels have even gotten up to full speed. Obviously, the actual spinning of the reels is window dressing since the outcome has already been predetermined.

By using this scheme, slot machines operate in a totally random fashion, and there isn't anything a player can do to change that. This is true for all currently-approved machines in legal casinos in the United States, whether they have video screens or spinning reels.

MACHINE PAYBACK

The average amount of money that a slot machine returns to the player after a long period of play is called the *payback*. The payback is stated as a percentage of the amount that the player invested in the machine. If the payback is 95%, for example, you can expect to lose five percent of every dollar that you bet.

Thus, the casino is charging you an average of five percent (over the long run) for the privilege of playing its machine. That is, for every dollar you risk, the casino keeps a nickel. That doesn't sound too bad, but in many cases the charge can be ten percent, or even twenty percent. The only thing that keeps this number from getting completely out of hand is the competition between casinos.

In the old days, by adjusting the number of symbols on the reels and by changing the payoff combinations, a slot machine could be made to pay back any desired percentage. Today, the payback is adjusted by changing a chip in the microprocessor, a procedure generally done at the slot machine factory. The payback usually ranges from 80% to 99%, except in New Jersey where, by law, slots have to pay back at least 83%. Keep in mind that these numbers are *long-term* averages.

Machines that are set to the lower end of the range are considered to be *tight*, while those at the upper end are *liberal* or *loose*.

In most major gaming jurisdictions, the average paybacks actually range from around 90 to 98%. Historically, the highest-paying machines have always been in Nevada, where Reno/Tahoe and North Las Vegas are usually in the lead, with downtown Las Vegas not far behind. The average paybacks on the Las Vegas strip run neck in neck with most smaller jurisdictions such as those in Mississippi, Louisiana, and Illinois. Atlantic City, taking advantage of the largest population center in the United States, trails behind by one to two points.

The average paybacks also vary according to the machine denomination. The more you are willing to risk, the more the casino is willing to give back. When a player switches to a higher denomination, the casino makes more money and can afford to give more of it back. The following chart shows the approximate average paybacks in Nevada for the year 2001 (rounded to the nearest point):

DENOMINATION	AVERAGE PAYBACK
Nickel	92%
Quarter	94%
Dollar	95%
$5	96%
$25	97%
$100	98%

Except for penny games (which we didn't bother listing), the nickel games still have the poorest payback, but that is beginning to change. Only a few years ago, the average for nickel payback was less than 90 percent. Nickel machines have changed dramatically with the proliferation of 45- and 90-credit video games.

The average bet per spin on a 45-coin nickel game is over a dollar, which makes these games more profitable for the casino than the quarter machines. Consequently, some casinos have been raising the paybacks on nickel games higher than their quarter slots. And before long, it is expected that the average payback for nickel games will exceed the quarter, and maybe even the half-dollar machines.

So why is the payback percentage important? Because

it has a direct effect on how fast your bankroll evaporates. Let's see how long a twenty-dollar bill will last in a machine that is running true to form, that is, neither hot nor cold. We can do this by theoretically running the twenty through the machine once and calculating the payback amount. (For this calculation, the machine denomination has no effect.) We then run the remainder through, calculating the payback on this new amount. In the following chart, we repeat the procedure 20 times:

PAYBACK PERCENTAGES			
Run No.	97%	92%	87%
Start	$20.00	$20.00	$20.00
1	$19.40	$18.40	$17.40
2	$18.82	$16.93	$15.14
3	$18.25	$15.57	$13.17
4	$17.71	$14.33	$11.46
5	$17.17	$13.12	$ 9.97
6	$16.66	$12.13	$ 8.67
7	$16.16	$11.16	$ 7.55
8	$15.67	$10.26	$ 6.56
9	$15.20	$ 9.44	$ 5.71
10	$14.75	$ 8.69	$ 4.97
15	$12.67	$ 5.73	$ 2.48
20	$10.88	$ 3.77	$ 1.23

At 97% payback, and after 20 run-throughs, we still have more than half of our original Jackson left. At 87%, however, we have barely enough left to tip the cocktail waitress. This plainly demonstrates that the payback percentage makes a significant difference.

Unlike video poker, however, there is no sure way to tell which slot machines are the best. The posted payout schedule on the machine is of little help without knowing how the microprocessor chip is programmed, which is information not readily available to the player. However, there are ways to offset this problem, which will be covered later.

THE ODDS OF HITTING
A JACKPOT

An interesting characteristic of most spinning reel slot machines is that regardless of the payback version of a particular machine, the odds of winning the top jackpot remain the same. The chances of hitting the top award is a function of how many different ways that symbol combination can occur out of the total number of possible symbol combinations programmed into the machine.

For a good illustration, we can look at the specifications for Diamonds & Roses, which is a popular Bally reel spinner. The two-coin version of this game is available in seven different paybacks from 83.41 to 97.09%. The top jackpot is 2500 coins, which can occur eight times out of a possible 373,248 symbol combinations. By dividing eight into 373,248, we see that the odds of hitting it works out to exactly one in 46,656 spins, slightly worse than the odds of hitting a natural royal flush in video poker.

The above paybacks are for a two-coin bet. The range of paybacks for a one-coin bet are 82.87 to 96.55%, which is only about half a percent less.

So how does the manufacturer change the overall machine payback without affecting the top jackpot? By adjusting the number of hits on some of the intermediate winning combinations. This is just as easy for the programmer and is better from a marketing standpoint. That is, it is better for marketing the machine to a casino, not to the players.

As a point of interest, no matter which version of this machine you play, the overall hit frequency is about 14.4%. This means you will hit some kind of payout an average of once every seven spins (100 ÷ 14.4 = 6.9).

Another interesting exercise is to calculate how many theoretical stops are on each reel. Since Diamonds & Roses is a three-reel machine, the number of stops per reel is the cube root of 373,248, which works out to be 72. Considering the limited physical size of a slot machine reel, it is not possible to fit on 72 stops. Each reel probably has 24 actual stops, which are then automatically multiplied three times by the program in the microprocessor.

FINDING THE LOOSEST SLOTS

Unlike video poker machines, you can't look at the payout schedule on a slot machine and tell if it is loose or tight. And when a casino advertises that its slots pay back *up to* 97% or that some of its slots have a "certified" 98% payback, it's difficult to tell which of the hundreds of machines on the floor are the advertised ones. Actually, you can get in the neighborhood, but it's not nearly as precise as finding the best video poker machines. The secret is (as they say in the real estate business)—location, location, location.

In every casino, the slot manager gives considerable thought to the placement of the slot machines. Therefore, to determine where the few loose slots are located on the casino floor, you have to think like the manager. An even better way is to get inside information directly from those slot managers—which is what we have done for you.

Years ago, it was generally known that the best slots were usually located in high-traffic areas—next to the main aisles or near the front entrance—where the greatest number of people would notice the flashing lights and ringing bells of a jackpot winner. Many old-time slot players remember that advice and still seek out machines in those locations. Times have changed, however.

Today, most slot managers place their loosest machines where the greatest number of *slot players* will see and hear them when they pay off. The idea is to motivate the serious slot players so they will keep feeding their machines in the hope that the next big jackpot will be theirs. Consequently, they locate the loose slots next to change booths, on elevated carousels, and anyplace in the center of the slot area where plenty of slot players will notice them when they pay off. Whenever loose slots are placed in a straight row of machines, they are usually one of the first three machines from either end, and never in the middle.

However, not all machines in these locations will be loose because there are always far fewer loose slots than tight ones. In fact, a typical ratio is 5 to 10% loose, 30 to 40% tight, with the remainder being mid-range. The best you can do is find the general area where most of the loose machines are likely to be.

Sometimes the managers also put a few loose slots within sight of the patrons in cafes and coffee shops (but not where the entrance line forms) to encourage players not to dally over their coffee, but to get back to their machines. Keep in mind, however, that tight slots always flank a loose slot, even though the machines appear to be identical. This is done to thwart those people who like to play two side-by-side machines simultaneously.

It is almost as important to know where the tight machines are likely to be placed by the slot manager, so you can avoid them. Anywhere people stand in lines waiting to get into buffets or shows, are prime locations for tight machines. Those people will kill time by idly dropping coins into the machines without really expecting to win—and they won't.

Because many table-game players are distracted and annoyed by the constant clatter of coins, the areas surrounding the table games (especially baccarat and roulette) are populated with tight machines. The same is true of areas near the sportsbook. In fact, any location where the noise of slot machines would disturb non-slot players is apt to have predominately tight machines.

Finally, you must assume that all slot machines located outside of casinos, such as in convenience stores, grocery stores, laundromats, airports, bars, and restaurants, are very tight. In fact, they are probably the tightest machines in town.

PAYBACK CYCLES

During relatively short periods of play, the actual payback of a machine may be significantly higher or lower than the long-term average. Since you probably play a given machine for only a few hours at a time, your concern is for short-term rewards, while the casino is interested in long-term profits.

Consequently, from a short-term viewpoint, a slot machine is considered *hot* when it is paying out more than expected, and it is considered *cold* when it is paying less than expected. It is widely believed that most machines, regardless of how loose or tight they are to begin with, go through hot cycles and cold cycles. Thus, a hot tight machine is better than a cold loose one. In the next section, we explain how to judge whether a machine is currently running hot or cold.

TESTING YOUR MACHINE

Once you have found a suitable non-progressive machine, it is prudent to first run a simple test to judge whether it is hot or cold.

Do this by playing through one roll of 40 quarters ($10) allowing the winnings to collect in the tray or accumulate as credits. In a two-coin machine, this will amount to 20 spins. In a three-coin machine, you will get 13 spins, with an odd coin left over.

When the roll is finished, count the number of coins that have collected in the tray, or look at how many credits you have accumulated. If your winnings are at least 75% ($7.50) of what you invested, stick with the machine. If not, move to another machine and repeat the test. Of course, in a dollar machine, your investment will be four times as large, but the testing principle remains the same.

In any case, if after the first six spins of the test you have won nothing, the machine is cold, and you should vacate it without carrying the test any further.

If your test winnings are at least 75%, but less than 90%, the machine is marginal and you may want to repeat the test to find out if it's in an *up cycle* or *down cycle*. Should the second test turn out better than the first, the machine is probably in an up cycle. This means the machine is getting hotter, and you should stick with it. Otherwise, abandon the machine. This test does not determine how loose or tight a machine is, but only if it is running hot or cold. Even tight machines have hot cycles.

Keep in mind that a hot cycle has a limited life, even on a loose machine. Consequently, you should be prepared to quit a hot machine as soon as it appears to be turning cold. An important clue is that it hasn't paid off in six consecutive spins. In fact, the most conservative players will abandon their machine after five cold spins.

This testing procedure only applies to basic flat-pay machines, and not to progressives. The strategy with progressive slot machines is to go for the main jackpot, with little concern for smaller wins, as explained in *Beating the Progressives* chapter.

SPINNING REEL SLOTS

On the surface, many reel spinners still look similar to slot machines installed in the early Las Vegas casinos over a half century ago. They have three spinning reels, and some of them still have a pull-handle on the right side, just like the old one-armed bandits.

Inside the cabinet, however, they are totally different. They may have mechanical reels, but those reels are driven by electric stepper motors that are fully controlled by a microprocessor. The pull-handle, which used to engage gears and cams that mechanically spun the reels, now simply operates an electrical switch connected to the same circuit as the switch under the SPIN button.

Many progressive machines are also reel spinners, but this section only covers games with a static (unchanging) top jackpot.

Although the variety of spinning reel machines may seem endless, they come in just four main flavors. All other differences have to do with the kinds of symbols used and the amounts of the payouts.

Following are the four basic types:

1. COIN MULTIPLIERS

In most casinos, *multipliers* are very popular machines. Multipliers are single-payline games where the number of coins bet on one spin multiplies the potential payouts. When this mathematical relationship is exact, we call the game a **true multiplier**.

In most games, however, the top jackpot is higher than the multiple when the maximum number of coins is bet. We call this version a **modified multiplier** (see illustration). The purpose of a modified multiplier is to encourage the player to bet the maximum on every spin. For instance, on most three-coin multipliers, if the top jackpot pays 1000 coins for a one-coin bet, the second coin will pay 2000 coins, but the third coin may pay 4000 coins (instead of 3000 coins), or even 5000 coins or more. The conventional advice is to always bet the maximum number of coins. However, this is not necessarily good advice, as we will explain later.

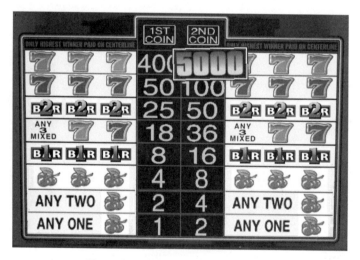

Typical modified multiplier paytable

2. MULTI-LINE GAMES

As you stroll through the casinos, you will notice that there are plenty of reel spinners with multiple paylines. In the industry, they are called *line games* because the paytable is payline-driven. While a single payline slot has one horizontal line across the window, a three-payline slot has two extra horizontal lines, one above and one below the center line. The extra paylines are activated by betting additional coins, giving you two additional chances of hitting a winning combination. Although you may activate one, two, or three of the paylines by inserting one, two, or three coins, to qualify for the maximum jackpot benefit, you must play all three coins.

Some machines have five paylines, with two of them criss-crossing the window diagonally, giving you a total of five winning chances (see illustration). These machines take up to five coins, one for each payline, and here again, you must play the maximum number of coins to qualify for the top jackpot. From the standpoint of return on investment, the multi-line slots are perfectly

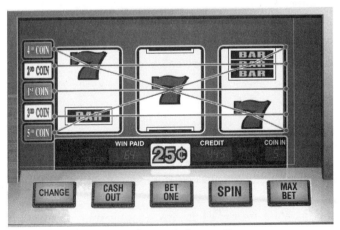

Slot window with five paylines

fine machines if you don't mind the higher bankroll requirement.

When looking for a game to play, don't assume all machines with the same name are identical. The IGT game called Triple Diamond comes in several versions that have one, three, five, or nine paylines. Furthermore, the one-payline version comes as a two-coin or three-coin multiplier.

3. OPTION-BUY GAMES

Option-buy games are usually (but not always) single-payline games that may be called Buy-Your-Pay or Buy-A-Pay, as well as various disparaging names. When you bet more than one coin, instead of multiplying the payout, these machines activate additional winning symbol combinations (see illustration). To get all the possible winning combinations, you must play the maximum number of coins. Unless you do so, the overall payback of the machine is seriously compromised.

Some three-coin option-buy games can be misleading because the second coin is a multiplier, and only the third coin buys you additional symbol combinations. Therefore, on any game you are considering, study the paytable carefully because if is an option-buy, you must never bet less than the maximum.

So why would anyone call an option-buy game bad names? Because many people do not read the paytable carefully, and then they get angry when they bet one coin, hit a winning combination of symbols, and get paid *absolutely nothing*. If it was a multiplier, they would have been paid a reduced amount, but they would have won *something*. Most people tend to get upset when they finally hit a winner and then don't get paid. Don't let this happen to you. If you decide to play an option-buy game, be sure you always bet the maximum.

Typical option-buy paytable

4. BANKING GAMES

These are games in which points, credits, or some form of game assets are accumulated as they are played. They are designed to encourage players to continue playing until they eventually collect the banked bonus. Banking games may also have the paytable features of multipliers or line games.

Although some banking games, such as Piggy Bankin' and X-Factor, are reel spinners, more and more of them are video games with secondary bonus screens. The best strategy for profitably playing reel spinning banking games is basically the same as for the video versions. To keep all the detailed playing information for banking games together, the playing strategy for reel spinning versions is included with the video versions in *Beating the Video Slots* chapter.

VIDEO VERSIONS OF SPINNING REEL GAMES

The major slot machine manufacturers, such as IGT and Bally, provide some of their most popular machines in either a spinning reel or video format. These are three-reel slots and, except for the format, both versions are identical. They are either multipliers, multi-line, or option-buy machines, so the information in this chapter applies to the video versions as well as the spinning reel versions.

Following are a few examples of slots that are marketed in both formats:

> Blazing 7s
> Double Diamond
> Red, White & Blue
> Sizzling 7s
> Triple Diamond
> White Lightning

BEATING THE SPINNING REELS

When most slot machine players take a vacation at a gambling resort, they allocate a certain amount of money for gambling. We refer to this allocated money as their *bankroll* or *stake*. Some of the players lose their bankroll by the end of the first day. Some of them are able to stretch their bankroll to the end of their vacation. Some of them come home money ahead. It appears that some people are just lucky and others are not.

This may be true, but if the same people almost always lose and other people almost always win, there must be more than luck involved. The difference is that some people play haphazardly without thinking, while others play thoughtfully and methodically. Is there a thoughtful way to play a seemingly mindless game such as slots? You bet there is—and in the following sections we suggest some shrewd and intelligent ways to improve your chances of coming out ahead.

STUDY THE GLASS

On a reel spinner, the paytable (known as the *glass*) is prominently posted above the reels. You should carefully examine this paytable before you actually start to play any machine. You may be surprised to note how different the payouts are from machine to machine, especially how much the top jackpot changes. Two side-by-side machines that appear to be basically identical (say, two-coin, one payline) may have top jackpots of 2500 coins and 10,000 coins, respectively. Although it might seem better to play the one with the highest jackpot, to compensate for that jackpot, it will have fewer small and medium payouts. The overall paybacks of the two machines may, in fact, be very similar.

So which machine should you play? If you select the one with the large jackpot, you can't worry too much about small wins, because you are going for the big one. Just try not to be too disappointed when you don't hit it, because that top jackpot is at least as elusive as a royal flush in video poker. If you select a machine with a smaller top jackpot, your bankroll will last longer and fluctuate less because it will be regularly replenished with small and medium wins. We think you will be more satisfied with such a machine.

Finally, before you start to play, check the glass to be sure you didn't inadvertently choose an option-buy game. This type of machine is not always obvious; especially those versions where the option-buy feature only applies to the last coin. If you really do want to play an option-buy game, be sure to read the section below on Multi-Line and Option-Buy Machines.

COIN MULTIPLIERS
Choose a Simple Machine

The strategy used by experienced players when selecting a spinning reel slot is to stick to the basic three-reel non-progressive machines. This is also the best advice for novice players. To stretch your bankroll, look for two-coin machines with a single payline. By sticking with a single-payline machine, you will know, without studying the paytable, that you are playing either a multiplier or an option-buy game. By betting maximum coins or credits on a two-coin machine, you know that you will always qualify for the top awards. Therefore, for inexperienced players, this is the safest approach for a minimum investment.

If you find the paytables to be even the slightest bit confusing, heed the above advice. The more sophisticated techniques outlined below require you to fully understand the paytables for the various types of games. If you are looking for more variety, there is nothing wrong with playing the three- and five-coin machines, so long as you have a sufficient bankroll that allows you to always bet the maximum. Just remember that doing so will deplete your bankroll more quickly.

Avoid Games with High Jackpots

Somehow this sounds contrary to what we are trying to do. Don't we want to win the biggest jackpots? Sure, but the chances of being successful are extremely remote. For example, a very popular Bally game is Stars & Bars. One version of this game has a top jackpot of 10,000 coins, but the chances of winning it are 1 out of 262,144 spins. It doesn't take a math genius to figure out that at 400 spins per hour, you would have to play over 655 hours to rack up 262,144 spins.

There is another version of Stars & Bars with a top jackpot of only 1200 coins, but the chances of winning are much better: 1 out of 32,768 spins. In this case, the lower the payout, the better the chance of winning it.

As we examine the specifications for different models of machines, we find this to be a general trend. Take a *really* high jackpot, such as the 40,000 coins found on French Quarters (50,000 in some versions). Here the chances of winning the top award are 1 in 2,097,152 spins! This is getting to be astronomical for a non-progressive game. Of course, there is a mathematical reason why the program designers have to do this: to control the overall payback on the machine, these very high jackpots have to be made much tougher to hit.

This leads us to the logical and correct conclusion that, most of the time, it is easier to win the top prize in a game with smaller jackpots. Furthermore, to keep the overall payback balanced, many games with modest top awards will compensate by rewarding you with a greater number of small and medium payouts.

Therefore, our strategy advice is to play those games with the lower jackpots, preferably no higher than 3000 coins. This has another advantage: Most slot players go for machines with high jackpots, so the ones with low jackpots are more likely to be available in a crowded casino. In the next section we advise you to look for true multipliers, and these games almost always have low to modest jackpots.

Bet One Coin Per Spin

"But everyone says I should always bet the maximum coins to be sure I qualify for the main jackpots. In fact,

you just said that a few paragraphs earlier." Yes, we did. But that advice was for inexperienced players and those who would rather not walk around the casino studying paytables.

We disagree with the advice to bet the maximum when it is given as a blanket rule. You will actually be money ahead by betting only one coin when you play certain machines, such as a true or near-true multiplier with a relatively-low top jackpot (see illustration). This is the case even if you do eventually win that jackpot, which is a remote possibility.

Typical true multiplier paytable

Betting a single coin on a three-coin machine cuts your monetary risk to one-third of what it would have been with a maximum bet. Such an approach may also allow you to move to a higher denomination, and higher denomination machines are generally a little looser. Thus, by applying some judgment in selecting your machine, you could get a better overall return by betting only a single coin or credit.

Although true multipliers may be somewhat scarce in some casinos, you shouldn't have much trouble finding a near-true multiplier. There are usually plenty of them around. These are machines where the maximum bet jackpot is only slightly greater than the coin multiple.

The following chart gives some examples of what you should be looking for.

EXAMPLES OF
TRUE AND NEAR-TRUE MULTIPLIERS

IGT GAMES

Game	Coin	1st	2nd	3rd	Type
Double Diamond	3	800	1600	2500	Near True
Purple Passion	2	800	1600		True
Purple Passion	3	800	1600	2500	Near True
Spin Til You Win	2	500	1000		True
Triple Diamond	2	1000	2500		Near True
Triple Diamond	3	5000	10,000	15,000	True

BALLY GAMES

Game	Coin	1st	2nd	3rd	Type
California Dreamin'	2	800	1600		True
California Dreamin'	3	800	1600	2500	Near True
Diamond Winners	3	1000	2000	4000	Near True
Double Trouble	2	800	1600		True
Triple Gold	2	1000	2500		Near True
Wild Rose	2	800	1600		True

The 1st Coin, 2nd Coin, and 3rd Coin columns show the top jackpot for those games. Lesser payouts for all the listed games are exact multiples of the number of coins bet. Be careful when you check the paytables because some true and near-true multipliers also come in option-buy versions.

MULTI-LINE AND OPTION-BUY MACHINES
Avoid games with high jackpots

Avoiding high jackpots is the same advice we gave above for multipliers. It applies equally to multi-payline and option-buy games, and the justification is the same as for multipliers.

Always Bet the Maximum

Both multi-payline and option-buy machines penalize the player for not making a maximum bet, some more than others. Therefore, if you insist on playing these games, always bet the maximum, which in most cases will be two, three, or five credits. If you don't do this, you will be penalizing yourself.

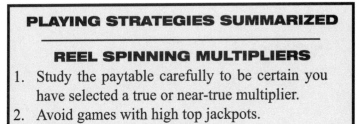

PLAYING STRATEGIES SUMMARIZED

REEL SPINNING MULTIPLIERS

1. Study the paytable carefully to be certain you have selected a true or near-true multiplier.
2. Avoid games with high top jackpots.
3. Bet one coin or credit per spin.

PLAYING STRATEGIES SUMMARIZED

MULTI-LINE AND
OPTION-BUY MACHINES

1. Avoid games with high top jackpots.
2. Always bet the maximum.

VIDEO SLOT MACHINES

The newest and glitziest slot machines on the casino floors display five or six simulated reels on a video screen. Although these games typically have nine to fifteen paylines, there are some with up to forty paylines that zigzag in almost every conceivable direction across the screen. On most machines, a bonus mode appears on a secondary screen when you hit the right symbol combinations. This bonus mode is the only real chance you have to recoup your losses and get ahead of the game. Other machines have a bonus banking mode to encourage you to keep playing in an attempt to reach the big bonus payout before your bankroll is totally depleted.

The most common games, however, have five reels, nine paylines, and encourage you to bet up to five coins per line. Because this adds up to 45 coins, a maximum bet on a quarter machine costs $11.25 a spin, which is too rich for most players. Consequently, the nickel machines have taken on new popularity. At $2.25 per spin, the maximum bet on a nickel version is all most players are ready to contend with. Yet the casinos continue to display their greediness by putting more and more ten-coin-per-line nickel machines on the main floor. At $4.50 for a maximum bet, these nickel games are competing with the $5 machines in the high-limit area. As you play any of these computerized wonders, keep in mind that when you bet 45 credits, and the machine noisily announces that you won 30 credits, *you are still losing money.*

Of course, none of this could happen if the nickel machines weren't more convenient to operate than they used to be. The days of buying rolls of nickels from the cashier and feeding them, one at a time, into the machine are gone. Now all you have to do is slip a bill into the currency acceptor and start to play. Of course, when you are ready to cash out, you still have to contend with that little coin bucket. Even this inconvenience is being overcome by machines that spit out credit tickets instead of coins.

Because most video games have multiple paylines and accept multiple coins for each payline, they might be called multiplier line games. And that they are, but within that designation there are two types of video games with distinctly different playing strategies. They are called *bonus games* and *banking games*. A third category, called *multi-game*, is a machine configuration that is important enough to be treated separately.

1. BONUS GAMES

Except for the video versions of spinning reel machines, almost all video games have secondary bonus screens that pop up when you hit certain symbol combinations. The bonus screens often require some action on the part of the player, and always result in the award of extra credits. Examples are:

Choose Your Bonus

Three to five objects appropriate to the game theme appear on the screen. By touching the screen, you select one of them, which then displays the number of credits you have won. An example is Bally's Boxcar Bonus.

Free Spins Bonus

A set of bonus reels with special symbols and multipliers appears on the screen. When the reels spin, a bonus is awarded for winning combinations, which may include additional bonus spins. An example is IGT's Elephant King.

Match Play Bonus

A bonus grid with hidden symbols appears on the screen. By touching the screen, you select grid spaces to find matching symbols and multipliers, which determine the amount of your bonus. An example is IGT's The Munsters.

Pick to Win Bonus

Items that hide bonus amounts are displayed on the screen. By touching the screen, you pick items that reveal bonus credits and multipliers. An example is WMS's Monopoly.

2. BANKING GAMES

To the casual observer, these appear to be ordinary bonus games, in that a secondary screen is part of the mix. There is, however, an important distinction that puts them in a class by themselves. As the game is played, points or some form of game assets are visibly accumulated by the machine in a "bank." When the bank reaches a certain condition or the achievement of some goal occurs as a result of continued play, these assets are finally paid out in the form of bonus credits.

This feature is designed to entice players to remain at the machine longer than they intended in an attempt to reach the payoff goal. Regardless of this enticement, some players may quit the game (for any number of reasons) before reaching the payoff goal. This leaves the game in a favorable state for any subsequent player who knows how to take advantage of it. Of course, we will tell you how to do it in the next chapter.

3. MULTI-GAME MACHINES

This is a configuration where the player has a choice of several different games within a single game machine. Most multi-game machines, such as Bally's Game Maker, include a mix of video slot games and video poker games. The video slot games may be of the bonus and/ or banking variety.

BEATING THE VIDEO SLOTS

The new video games are significantly different than the old spinning reel machines, so the best ways to play them are also different. Most video games use entertainment or personality themes to attract players. They may be based on television game shows such as Jeopardy or Wheel of Fortune, or they may be based on board games such as Monopoly or Bingo, or they may be pure inventions such as Reel 'Em In or Filthy Rich.

Whatever the case, try not to be influenced by the theme, but select a game on its potential first and entertainment value second.

BONUS GAMES

Except for the exact spinning reel emulators mentioned earlier in the *Spinning Reel Slots* chapter, most video slot machines have the bonus screen feature, and this includes the banking games. Banking games, however, require a different approach than ordinary bonus games, and are covered in the next section. To keep it as uncomplicated as possible, our strategy for bonus games covers only the most common types of machines, which are those with nine paylines and a maximum bet of either five or ten credits per payline (see illustration).

If you want to play a game with more paylines, try to apply the same basic principles we describe below.

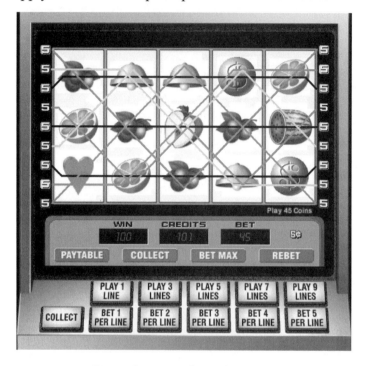

Five-reel, nine-payline video screen

Study the Paytable

Unlike spinning reel machines, the paytables on almost all video games are not posted on the outside of the cabinet. You must press a button to bring the schedule up on the screen, which is usually several pages in length. For this reason, most players never look at the paytable and play the game virtually blind. Unless you don't care about playing strategy, this is not a good way to go.

Before you start playing any new video game, it is always a good idea to first become familiar with the paytable. If nothing else, you should verify that the game is a true multiplier, that is, the payouts are multiplied by the number of credits bet and there is no special payoff benefit to playing the maximum number of lines and credits. This is the case for most of the games, but there are some that give a serious advantage for maximum bets. Avoid these because you lose all flexibility in your playing style.

To determine if a game is a true multiplier, look for statements on the paytable such as: **All Wins are Multiplied by the Credits Bet per Line** and **Scatter Wins are Multiplied by the Total Credits Bet.** There should be no statements that make exceptions for payouts on certain paylines.

Start With Three Paylines

The payline choices on most nine-payline games are one, three, five, seven, or nine lines. Unless you are an old hand, resist the urge to hit the MAX BET button, which will commit you to a bet of 90 credits on some machines! On a nickel machine, that amounts to $4.50 a spin. Even if your bankroll can handle higher denominations, until you get very familiar with these games, you should stick with the nickel machines.

To preserve your stake, never start by betting all nine lines. If you start with only one line, however, the payouts are so infrequent that you may get discouraged before you win anything. No matter what the machine denomination, it is best to start with one credit and three lines. On a nickel machine, this only amounts to 15¢, or 75¢ on a quarter machine.

If you are losing after a dozen spins, try another machine. If, however, you have accumulated some credits, then start betting five lines. If you continue winning, increase your bet to two credits, and so forth. You can play this way in an informal manner, or you can learn the betting sequence in the next section and use a more methodical approach.

Use An Incremental Betting Sequence

With so many choices of paylines and credits, you can make a total bet of as little as one credit or as much as 45 credits. On a ten-credits-per-payline machine, you can make a one-credit bet or a 90-credit bet. This leads to the idea of some form of systematic play to minimize risk and maximize gain, such as a Martingale doubling system. Those who would employ a Martingale, however, will be disappointed because there aren't enough steps available for it to work well.

The Martingale is usually applied to an even-money wager, such as the outside bets on a roulette wheel. It is designed to recoup previous losses with an eventual big win. The idea is that you start with a minimum bet and double it every time you lose. When you finally win, all losses are recovered (plus a small profit), and you then return to the original low bet to start the doubling procedure over again. This system has been applied to many games, including the slots.

The best we can do with the nine lines on a nickel machine, however, is shown in the following chart.

5¢ MACHINE - NINE LINES

LINES	CREDITS	TOTAL BET	AMOUNT
3	1	3	$0.15
3	2	6	$0.30
3	4	12	$0.60
5	5	25	$1.25
9	5	45	$2.25
9	10	90	$4.50

(This is an example only. It is not a recommended sequence.)

The problem with the above sequence is that there are only four doublings for 45 credits or five doublings for 90 credits to work with. From a practical standpoint, this is far from sufficient to effectively apply the system. A person wanting to pursue this line of thinking, however, might try making a similar chart for a twenty- or forty-payline machine.

What we do recommend is a similar system for recouping losses, except that the total bet is raised in a more gradual manner. Although the first step is unavoidably doubled in the betting sequence shown below, the subsequent increases are smoothly incremental, the span between steps being 3, 4, 5, 6, 7, 8, and 9 credits. As the chart shows, this progression for 45 credits has many more steps than the doubling system, and is easier to remember. The amount shown in the last column is the total cost per spin on a nickel machine.

RECOMMENDED SEQUENCE FOR 45 CREDITS - #1			
No. OF LINES	CREDITS PER LINE	CREDITS PER SPIN	TOTAL AMOUNT
3	1	3	$0.15
3	2	6	$0.30
5	2	10	$0.50
5	3	15	$0.75
7	3	21	$1.05
7	4	28	$1.40
9	4	36	$1.80
9	5	45	$2.25

A recommended way to apply the method is to start at the lowest betting level (3 lines, 1 credit per line). If you don't win anything, proceed to the next higher step by raising your bet to two credits per line. If you win just a small amount, say no more than triple your total bet (9 credits), repeat the bet. Only move to the next line if you have won nothing.

Continue working down the chart until you win an amount greater than three times your current bet. Whenever this happens, restart the betting sequence on the next spin by returning to the lowest betting level at the top of the chart.

The following is an example of a typical betting sequence.

TYPICAL BETTING SEQUENCE

No. of Lines	Credits/ Line	Credits/ Spin	Amt. of Win	Total Spent	Total Amt. Won
3	1	3	0	3	0
3	2	6	0	9	0
5	2	10	16	19	16
5	2	10	0	29	16
5	3	15	0	44	16
7	3	21	90	65	106
3	1	3	0	68	106
3	2	6	0	74	106
5	2	10	40	84	146
3	1	3	0	87	146
3	2	6	0	93	146
5	2	10	0	103	146
5	3	15	0	118	146
7	3	21	0	139	146
7	4	28	0	167	146
9	4	36	40	203	186
9	4	36	0	239	186
9	5	45	150	284	336
3	1	3	0	287	336
3	2	6	0	293	336
5	2	10	10	303	346
5	2	10	16	313	362
5	2	10	0	323	362
5	3	15	0	338	362
7	3	21	0	359	362
7	4	28	200	387	562

Eventually you will experience a losing streak that will run you to the bottom of the chart. In that case, you have no choice but to continue betting the maximum. Whenever you reach the 45 credit maximum bet without hitting a significant win, *don't stay there longer than one additional spin*. If you don't hit a decent payout by then, *cash out and walk away*.

If you are uncomfortable with betting 45 credits, end your sequence earlier, say at 36 credits. Just be aware that sooner or later you will reach whatever maximum you set for yourself and may have to stay there for a couple of spins.

As orderly as the above sequence is, there are two good reasons for increasing the number of credits per line faster than the number of lines. First, the chance of hitting a scatter pay is the same no matter how many paylines are activated, but the amount of the payout is determined by the number of credits bet. Second, when you get lucky and activate a bonus screen, those bonus amounts are also multiplied by the number of credits bet.

RECOMMENDED SEQUENCE FOR 45 CREDITS - #2

Number of Lines	Credits Per Line	Credits Per Spin	Total Amount
3	1	3	$0.15
3	2	6	$0.30
3	3	9	$0.45
3	4	12	$0.60
3	5	15	$0.75
5	5	25	$1.25
7	5	35	$1.75
9	5	45	$2.25

Many players seem to think they are better off activating all nine lines, and then try to preserve their bankroll by wagering only one credit. Yes, they will hit paying combinations more often, but the payoffs will be meager. For the same nine credits, betting three lines and three credits per line will usually be more fruitful.

Thus, I prefer the sequence in Chart 2, which is more irregular, but is easy to remember. Starting at three lines and one credit, increase the credits per line to two, three, four, and five, while staying at three lines. Then, while staying at five credits, increase the lines to five, seven, and nine.

Chart 2 is applied in exactly the same way as the Chart 1. Work your way down the chart until you win an amount greater than three times your current bet. Whenever this happens, restart the betting sequence on the next spin by returning to the lowest betting level at the top of the chart.

RECOMMENDED SEQUENCE FOR 90 CREDITS

Number of Lines	Credits Per Line	Credits Per Spin	Total Amount
3	1	3	$0.15
3	2	6	$0.30
5	2	10	$0.50
5	3	15	$0.75
7	3	21	$1.05
7	4	28	$1.40
9	4	36	$1.80
9	5	45	$2.25
9	6	54	$2.70
9	7	63	$3.15
9	8	72	$3.60
9	9	81	$4.05
9	10	90	$4.50

Now let's see what we can do with a 90-credit game. The problem with a 10-credit-per-line machine is that the number of credit buttons is limited to 1, 2, 3, 5, and

10 credits. If you want to bet 8 credits, you have to touch the 1 CREDIT button at the bottom of the screen eight times. So we're stuck with the following easy-to-remember but hard-to-use sequence, which is an extension of the first of the two recommended 45-credit tables above. Another solution is not to play the 90-credit games.

Finally, we should make clear that the betting sequences suggested above do not convey any particular mathematical advantage to the player. Although they are not a magic formula for beating the system, they do carry the following benefits that will help to preserve your bankroll, reduce your losses, and help you come out ahead.

FIVE ADVANTAGES OF USING THE BETTING SEQUENCES

1. Applying a predetermined betting sequence forces you to play in a more methodical manner, rather than aimlessly hitting the buttons as fast as you can.

2. This methodical approach reduces your playing speed, which helps to preserve your bankroll.

3. It also keeps your average betting level down, by having you start low and gradually increasing your bet. This reduces your overall investment risk.

4. The betting sequence helps to preserve larger wins by always making you return to the lowest betting level.

5. And most importantly, the methodical approach forces you to pay attention to the performance of the game so that you are more likely to stay with it when it is hot and abandon it when it goes cold.

BANKING GAMES

Being a special kind of bonus game, games with a banking feature can be played like other bonus games, as described above. However, they have a unique characteristic that, if taken advantage of, can result in overcoming the normal payback percentage built into the machine. This can happen when a previous player has left a banking machine in a state of increased value, either due to ignorance, a lack of funds, a pressing engagement, or some other reason. Another person, who recognizes the potential value of the machine, can then start to play it to advantage.

The advantage arises when some form of game assets have been saved or "banked" by the machine during a period of previous play. When the machine attains a certain condition or bonus goal as the result of resumed play, the accumulated assets are finally paid out in the form of credits. This will occur even if the resumed play is by a person other than the one who originally accumulated most of the banked assets.

The trick is to recognize when an abandoned machine has reached the point at which continued play will likely be profitable.

Search for Banked Credits

Video slot machines that have a banking feature are not always apparent. To the casual observer, most of them just look like ordinary bonus games. The banking feature, however, is described on the paytable (which you can see by touching the paytable button on the screen), and the feature usually becomes apparent when you start playing the game. Therefore, you can eventually find a banking game by walking from machine to machine, bringing up and reading the paytable on each one.

Reel spinning banking machines are a little more obvious. They always have a top box with some type of dot matrix graphic display. In any case, we save you some time and trouble by listing a number of the most common video and reel spinning banking games in the next section, along with suggestions as to when they have attained a profitable state.

Since the banking feature has been around for a few years, the potential value of banking games is known to many experienced slot players who have learned how to take advantage of them. Sadly, a few unscrupulous types have used techniques for encouraging a player to leave a machine when it reaches a valuable state. Casinos are aware of this and do not look kindly on such activities. Keep in mind that it is not good form to look over the shoulder of someone who is playing a banking slot, in the hope that they will abandon the game. Casinos generally don't care who plays their slot machines or who wins the bonuses, but they have been known to bar individuals who harass or annoy other slot players. And before you sit down at a machine, take a moment to assure that the machine has really been abandoned.

Before you actually start to play, study the paytable and playing directions very carefully. Some banking games get rather complicated in the way the bonuses are banked, so you need to know that you are playing correctly or you may lose the advantage that you started with.

MACHINES TO LOOK FOR

Useful information for playing some of the most popular banking games is provided below. Note that some of the listed banking games are reel spinners, which are included here because the strategy is basically the same as for the video banking games.

The playing advice is as current as we could make it, but be aware that manufacturers frequently modify their machines and you should try to verify that the game you are considering is the same one we describe.

Applying the following suggestions does not guarantee that you will be money ahead every time you play an advantageous machine, but only that your long-term average will be profitable.

BINGO

This is exactly like the game using cardboard bingo cards (you do know how to play bingo, don't you?). The video screen displays five reels that represent the five columns on a standard bingo card. Most of the time, the machine plays like any five-reel video game, but every so often a bingo ball appears on one of the columns and the machine will draw a bingo number. This continues until the selected bingo configuration is completed, whereupon a bonus round determines how many credits have been won.

Study the paytable to learn how to identify the various bingo configurations.

Strategy:
Bet one credit per spin on one payline if you find a game in which the bingo is at least half finished. Although Bingo has five paylines, the bingo ball does not have to fall on a line to be valid. Cash out when the banked bonus is won.

BOOM

This game banks firecrackers and awards the bonus when 50 are accumulated. Although it is a five credits-per-payline, nine-payline game, don't ever bet 45 credits.

Strategy:
Bet one credit on one payline when you find a game with at least 30 firecrackers lined up across the top of the screen. Cash out when the banked bonus is won.

BUCCANEER GOLD

This game, which is found on Odyssey machines, periodically enters a double-pay state. The onset of this state can be predicted by watching the rising rope at the left side of the screen until a flag unfurls. To take advantage of the short double-pay period, the game should be played as rapidly as possible until the period ends. The other banking feature is the accumulation of daggers in the lower right corner of the screen.

Strategy:
Bet three credits per spin when you find a game with at least three daggers. Cash out when the banked bonus is won.

CHUCK WAGONS

In this game of racing chuck wagons, if Your Wagon reaches the bonus area before Their Wagon finishes, you collect the banked bonus. The race distance is 70 miles.

Strategy:
Bet maximum credits per spin when you find a game in which Your Wagon has gone at least 30 miles and Their Wagon is at least 25% behind Your Wagon. Cash out when the banked bonus is won.

DIAMOND THIEF

This is a rather complex three-reel game with the ultimate goal of filling all nine compartments of a case with diamonds, six diamonds per compartment, for a total of 54 diamonds.

Strategy:
Bet one credit per spin when you find a game that needs no more than five diamonds to completely fill the case. Cash out when the banked bonus is won.

DOUBLE DIAMOND MINE, TRIPLE DIAMOND MINE

In these games, a bonus is paid when ten diamonds are accumulated in any of the three mineshafts.

Strategy:
Bet one credit per spin when you find a game with nine diamonds in one shaft, eight diamonds in two of the three shafts, or at least seven diamonds in each of all three shafts. Cash out when the game no longer meets any of the above three conditions.

EMPIRE, EMPIRE KING

In these games, King Kong has to climb the Empire State Building a certain number of stories within a certain time limit. In Empire, the first bonus level is 70 stories; in Empire King, the bonus level is 90 stories. Study the paytable to get the details.

Strategy:
Bet the maximum credits per spin when you find a game with at least twice as many seconds left on the timer as there are stories remaining for King to climb. Cash out when the distance counter resets to zero.

FISHIN' FOR CASH

This is a fishing version of Double Diamond Mine. Whenever a fish appears on the payline, it is reeled in and piled on one of three stacks.

Strategy:
Bet one credit per spin when you find a game with nine fish in one stack, eight fish in two of the three stacks, or at least seven fish in each of all three stacks. Cash out when the game no longer meets any of the above three conditions.

FORT KNOX

In this Odyssey game, the banked items are the numerical digits of the combination to a vault. When you finally get all of the digits, the vault opens and you are paid the amount residing in one of three safety deposit boxes.

Strategy:
Bet the maximum credits per spin when you find a game that has at least five digits of the combination already revealed. In newer versions of the game, the number of digits that have been previously obtained cannot be seen without playing one spin. You get around this by inserting a coin or bill while the machine is in the menu mode, and then calling up the game. If you don't like what you see, cash out, and it has cost you nothing. If you decide to play, cash out when a new combination is formed.

GREASED LIGHTNING

This is a version of Chuck Wagons, where '57 Chevys are raced instead of chuck wagons.

Strategy:
Bet maximum credits per spin when you find a game in which Your Car has gone at least 30 miles and Their Car is at least 25% behind Your Car. Cash out when the banked bonus is won.

ISLE OF PEARLS

This is a variation of Empire where you go down instead of up. To get the bonus, a pearl diver needs to descend at least 70 feet before time runs out (100 seconds).

Strategy:
Bet the maximum credits per spin when you find a game where the diver has gone at least 30 feet and there are at least twice as many seconds left on the timer as there are feet remaining for the diver to descend. Cash out when it is obvious that the diver will not reach 70 feet before the time runs out.

JUNGLE KING

This is the opposite of Isle of Pearls, where the Jungle Man needs to climb up a vine a distance of 70 feet within 100 seconds.

Strategy:

Bet the maximum credits per spin when you find a game where there are at least twice as many seconds left on the timer as there are feet remaining for Jungle Man to climb. Cash out when the distance counter resets to zero.

LADY OF FORTUNE

In this Odyssey game, the banked items are the 12 letters and symbols in the phrase +BONUSxROUND. Each time one of them appears in the gypsy's crystal ball, it lights up, and when all 12 are illuminated, you have reached the bonus round.

Strategy:

Bet the maximum credits per spin when you find a game in which at least 6 of the 12 letters/symbols are already illuminated. Note that the maximum bet may be two or three credits, depending on the version of the machine. Cash out when the bonus is won.

MERLIN

This is another clone of Empire with Merlin trying to reach a castle before time runs out.

Strategy:

Bet the maximum credits per spin when you find a game with at least twice as many seconds left on the timer as there are units remaining for Merlin to travel. Cash out when the distance counter resets to zero.

PIGGY BANKIN'

Piggy Bankin' was the original banking game, and it caused quite a stir among the experts and analysts when this three-reel machine was first introduced. It also established WMS Gaming as a major competitor in the slot machine business.

Strategy:

In Piggy Bankin', whenever you get three blank spaces on the payline, your bet is added to the contents of a piggy bank. Then, when the Break the Bank symbol lands on the right-hand payline, the contents of the piggy bank are yours. *Bet one credit per spin when you find a $1, $2, or $5 game with at least 25 credits, or a nickel or quarter game with at least 30 credits in the bank.* Cash out when you break the bank.

BIG BANG PIGGY BANKIN'

Big Bang Piggy Bankin' is a newer version of the Piggy Bankin' game (above).

Strategy:

In Big Bang Piggy Bankin', you have to get three Break the Bank symbols (or wild equivalents) to win the banked bonus. *Bet one credit per spin when you find a game with at least 50 credits in the bank.* Cash out when you break the bank.

RED BALL

This three-payline nickel machine displays two 3 by 3 matrix squares alongside the video reels. The idea is to fill one of the squares with red balls and the other with black balls. Under each square is a number indicating the amount of the payoff bonus for completing that square.

Strategy:

Bet one credit per line per spin (a total of three credits) when you find a game with at least a 20 under either square or at least a 15 under both. Cash out when the game no longer meets the above conditions.

SHOPPING SPREE

This game banks frequent shopper points, and the banked bonus is paid when 50 points are accumulated.

Strategy:

Bet two credits per spin when you find a game with at least 30 frequent shopper points already registered. Cash out when you win the bonus.

SUPER 7s

This five-payline game is found on Game King machines, and the banked items are square sevens, that is, each seven is inside of a square.

Strategy:

Bet one credit per line per spin (a total of five credits) when you find a game with at least three square sevens showing. Cash out when you win the bonus.

TEMPERATURE'S RISING

The idea is to raise the temperature on a large red thermometer to the bonus level. The heat goal depends on the particular machine version, but is plainly shown.

Strategy:

Bet one credit per spin when you find a game where the amount of the bonus is greater than the number of degrees needed to "break" the thermometer. Cash out when the bonus is won.

TRIPLE CASH WINFALL

This is a money version of Double Diamond Mine, where coins fall on one of three stacks.

Strategy:

Bet one credit per spin when you find a game with nine coins in one stack, eight coins in two of the three stacks, or at least seven coins in each of all three stacks. Cash out when the game no longer meets any of the above three conditions.

TRIPLE DIAMOND BASEBALL DIAMOND

Ball players move around the bases as you hit a single, double, triple, or home run on the third reel of this machine. The runs are accumulated and are paid out when you get a home run.

Strategy:

Bet one credit per spin when you find a game with at least 25 accumulated runs plus the runs shown over the base runner's heads. Cash out when the base runners are cleared by a home run.

WILD CHERRY PIE, WILD CHERRY BONUS PIE

Through a rather convoluted process, a total of 54 cherries have to be accumulated in a nine-section pie.

Strategy:
For Wild Cherry Pie, bet one credit per spin when you find a game with at least 44 cherries in the large pie. For Wild Cherry Bonus Pie, bet one credit per spin when you find a game with at least 48 cherries in the large pie. Cash out when the pie is filled and the bonus is paid.

X-FACTOR

The X factor is a payout multiplier that starts at 2X and can build as high as 10X. Whenever you choose to use the multiplier, it resets to 2X.

Strategy:
Bet the maximum credits per spin when you find a game with an X factor of at least 6X. Cash out when the multiplying factor has been used.

MULTI-GAME MACHINES

Nearly all casinos have plenty of multi-game machines on the floor. The most popular are Bally's Game Maker, IGT's Game King, and Anchor's Winning Touch. Although Silicon Gaming no longer exists as a company, its Odyssey machines are still prevalent in many casinos. Each of these machines contains a variety of choices, which usually includes a mix of video poker and video slot games.

Many of the games listed above can be found on multi-game machines such as Game King and Odyssey, machines which are almost entirely touch-screen driven. Before committing any currency, you can surf your way through numerous screens to get instructions and paytable information on every game it contains.

In addition to video poker, most of the selections will likely be video bonus games and video versions of reel spinners. Use the playing strategies described earlier for these games. If the menu contains a banking game, by using the suggestions in the previous section, you can determine ahead of time if it is worth playing.

PLAYING STRATEGIES SUMMARIZED

VIDEO BONUS GAMES

1. Bring up the paytable and check that the game is a true multiplier.
2. Start with 3 paylines and 1 credit per line.
3. On each subsequent spin, increase the paylines or the credits by a single increment.
4. When a win exceeds triple your current bet, return to 3 lines and 1 credit on the next spin, restarting the sequence.

VIDEO BANKING GAMES

1. Look for banking games with some credits already banked.
2. Play the game according to the advice given in the section on Banking Games.

PROGRESSIVE SLOTS

In progressive slot machines the top jackpot is not fixed. Progressives are usually part of a linked group of machines, and as the individual slots are played, the jackpot continually grows until someone wins it. After a win, the jackpot is reset to a base value and then begins to grow again. Some players are unaware that there is often a secondary jackpot, which is much smaller than the primary.

Progressive slots are typically 2-, 3-, or 5-coin machines, although some video nickel machines will take as many as 45 coins. In every case, the maximum number of coins must be bet to qualify for the top prize. Because progressives require a larger bankroll than basic flat pays, we don't recommend them for beginning slot players. The looseness or tightness of a progressive machine is entirely dependent on the current jackpot amount, since that determines the overall payback.

Progressive slot machines can be divided into three distinct categories. The categories roughly define how many machines are linked together (if any), and how large the progressive jackpots grow. As we will see later, the playing strategies for all the categories are quite similar.

STAND-ALONE PROGRESSIVES

At one time, all progressive slot machines were stand-alone. That was before someone thought of the idea of linking progressives together to make the jackpot meter tick up faster and higher. Most casinos still have stand-alones, the big difference being that the progressive jackpot is in the thousands of dollars instead of the hundreds of thousands or millions.

Generally you can identify a stand-alone by the lack of a large jackpot meter above the row or carousel. Instead, there is a meter on each individual machine, which doesn't change unless someone is playing the game.

LOCAL PROGRESSIVES

The first linked progressives were groups of machines within a single casino that were connected together so that they all contributed to a common jackpot pool. The size of a particular progressive group may be as small as a half dozen machines or as large as several dozen. Each cluster of machines has a large meter that displays the current value of the jackpot.

You can tell it isn't a WAPS (see below) because the jackpot will be in the tens of thousands. If you are not sure, just ask an attendant or a floor supervisor.

WIDE AREA PROGRESSIVE
SLOTS (WAPS)

These are the big money progressive machines. In 1986, IGT set up the first citywide linked progressive machines in Las Vegas and called them Megabucks. They were so successful that dozens of wide-area progressive systems have been started since then—the majority being operated by IGT. On most of them, the top jackpot runs into the millions, and that accounts for their enormous popularity.

The idea of linking hundreds of similar machines within a single gaming jurisdiction such as Nevada or New Jersey has resulted in very high payouts and frequent winners.

The individual casinos do not own the wide area machines. They are installed and maintained by a system operator such as IGT. When IGT sets up a new Megabucks machine, all the casino does is provide the floor space and take its cut of the action. IGT maintains the machine and all associated equipment including the interconnecting telephone lines. They handle all the needed administration and promotional activities, in addition to verifying and paying all the jackpots.

BEATING THE PROGRESSIVES

The vast majority of progressive players are primarily interested in winning the top jackpot. These players consider the smaller wins to be useful only for replenishing their bankrolls so they can stay at their machines for a longer period of time. To support the large progressive jackpots, the machines are programmed so that the medium and small wins occur less often than in non-progressive games. If you have this all-or-nothing mentality, then the progressives are your game.

STRATEGY FOR STAND-ALONE AND LOCAL PROGRESSIVES

If you like the idea of big jackpots but would prefer something less elusive than what the wide area progressives offer, you might be interested in trying a local bank of progressives. If the amount on the progressive meter is less than $100,000, then it is almost certainly a local group, unless it is Bally's Blondie, which has a rather low reset of $25,000.

If you are not sure if a particular row or carousel is local or WAPS, ask a floor supervisor. One advantage to playing a stand-alone or local progressive is that the jackpot will be paid in a lump sum.

Look for High Jackpots

The only strategy is to find a linked group of machines that is displaying a high amount on the progressive meter. This is not difficult because the present value of the top jackpot is prominently displayed on a large digital sign above each bank of machines, the number continually ticking upward as the players insert coins. If there is a secondary jackpot, it is shown on a smaller meter below the top jackpot sign.

Each time the jackpot is won, the amount on the meter is reset to a base value. Whenever a progressive meter is close to the base amount, it means there was a recent win and the next win is not likely to occur for some time. You should always try to find a group of machines where the meter shows the greatest dollar increment over the reset value. To find out what that reset value is, you will have to ask a supervisor. Just remember that when you play *any kind* of progressive, you must always bet the maximum if you expect to qualify for the big jackpot.

Then there are those individual stand-alone machines with progressive jackpots that are often no higher than many of the non-progressive slots. There doesn't seem to be any valid reason to play these machines. If you do, be sure to find one in which the jackpot has been run up by other players, and bet the maximum.

Bet the Maximum Coins or Credits

No matter what else you might do, when playing a progressive *always bet the maximum*. It is the only chance you have of beating the system. If you don't bet the maximum coins or credits, you cannot win the progressive jackpot—and if you don't have a crack at the top jackpot, the overall payback on the machine will be rather poor. If you don't want to risk that much money, you are playing the wrong machine and you should find one of a lower denomination. Or you shouldn't be playing progressives at all.

STRATEGY FOR WIDE AREA PROGRESSIVE SLOTS (WAPS)

The jackpots on WAPS, which can be a lifestyle-changing amount of money, are seldom won—so seldom that when someone gets lucky, it is always reported in the newspaper. WAPS have to be approached with a totally different attitude; that is, you can't mind blowing your entire bankroll on the infinitesimal chance of hitting a gigantic payday.

It's something like playing the state lottery on a continuous basis. And you know what they say about most state lotteries: Your chances of winning the big one are statistically the same whether or not you buy a ticket.

Furthermore, besides feeding a percentage of the receipts to the progressive jackpot escrow account, both the WAPS operator (such as IGT or Bally) and the casino in which the machine is located, take their cut. Consequently, the overall payback to the player is always less than 90%, often much less.

For this reason, *we don't recommend playing them.* The odds of winning the progressive jackpot itself are so poor that every time you hit the SPIN or MAX BET button, you are literally throwing your money down a black hole. How can this be any fun?

For those of you who still insist on playing these machines, be sure you always bet the maximum coins or credits, or you will have a zero chance of winning the top jackpot. Although some WAPS have been known to hit just above the reset amount, we still recommend that you wait until the progressive meter gets at least twice as high.

We do hate to encourage you, but will provide some basic information on the most popular progressives that can be found in most jurisdictions.

Megabucks

The mother of all WAPS, these dollar slots have been around since IGT installed the first ones in 1986. The first Megabucks progressive jackpot was hit on February 1st, 1987 in Reno, Nevada for nearly five million dollars. These machines may be found in most casinos within each major gambling jurisdiction such as Nevada and Mississippi, as well as in Tribal casinos. All the machines in a given jurisdiction are linked to the same huge jackpot pool.

Megabucks is usually a three-coin, four-reel machine, so you have to invest $3 on each spin to qualify for the primary jackpot. Line up the four Megabucks symbols on the payline and you win a multi-million dollar jackpot that is paid out in annual installments. After a win, the primary jackpot is reset to $7 million (in Nevada), and the secondary jackpot is reset to $2000. Over the past two years, the Megabucks top jackpot has been hit eight times in Nevada with payouts ranging from $7,671,788 to $34,955,490.

In 1990, IGT set up a Megabucks WAPS network in Atlantic City. It never was very profitable for the operators, which some analysts blamed on the nature of the Eastern gaming market. For many years, in an attempt to improve revenues, IGT did some serious adjusting and fiddling. They changed the number of reels and raised the reset amount, but they could never find the formula for success. In 2002, they finally gave up and shut down the system. In Nevada, however, Megabucks has never been more popular.

Wheel of Fortune

Another IGT success story, this three-reeler is now the most popular of all WAPS. It comes in four denominations, and requires the maximum number of coins to win the progressive, as follows:

Quarters . . .   Three coin max bet and $200,000 reset.
Halves . . . .   Three coin max bet and $500,000 reset.
Dollars . . . .   Two coin max bet and $1 million reset.
Five dollars .   Two coin max bet and $1 million reset.

The record jackpot of $9,866,728 was hit in Mississippi on a one-dollar machine. The smallest primary payout was $200,006 on a quarter machine, barely more than the reset. The top payouts are made in annual installments for all denominations, which is common for IGT machines.

Wheel of Fortune Video

The video version has five simulated reels and is found in most jurisdictions except Nevada. It comes in nickel and quarter denominations. The record jackpot of just over $3 million was won on a nickel machine at a Tribal casino in Wisconsin.

Betty Boop's Big Hit

This is Bally's most popular WAPS, and it has some unusual features. First, most of the machines are multi-denominational; you feed a bill into the currency acceptor and then decide if you want to play nickels, quarters, or dollars. Second, in one carousel there are usually several theme variations, such as Swing Time Betty, Betty Boop's Double Jackpot, and Betty Boop's Roaring 20s.

To qualify for the progressive jackpot, you have to bet five nickels, three quarters, or two dollars. If you think you can beat the system by betting just five nickels, think again. According to Bally, the machines are programmed so that a player who bets two dollars has an eight times better chance of hitting the top jackpot than the player who risks only 25 cents by betting five nickels.

Furthermore, the overall theoretical payback rises as the denomination goes up: 84%, 86%, and 88% for nickels, quarters, and dollars, respectively. After someone hits the progressive, the machines reset to $100,000, and the winner is immediately paid the entire jackpot (less taxes).

Quartermania

As the name implies, this IGT WAPS accepts quarters, although it takes two of them to qualify for the big payoff, which is paid in twenty annual installments. The primary reset is $1 million, while the secondary is restarted at a measly $1000. The record jackpot of $3,778,205 was hit way back in July 1997. Since then, the primary progressive wins in Nevada have ranged from $1,016,941 to $2,197,872.

Jeopardy

Jeopardy is basically a quarter machine except in Atlantic City where there are also fifty-cent and dollar versions. The quarter version, which takes three coins and resets to $200,000, has paid out as much as $8 million in Louisiana. This is another IGT machine, so it pays the top jackpot in annual installments.

Jeopardy Video

Jeopardy also comes in a video version. It is a nickel machine with a reset of $100,000. Because you have to bet 45 credits to qualify for the progressive payout, it is more expensive to play than the non-video three-reel version. The record jackpot of $2,188,462 was paid as a lump sum in Atlantic City, which is the one advantage to this game.

Elvis

This is another popular three-reel IGT game, which sports a bonus feature that plays Elvis tunes. It comes in two denominations with the following specifications:

Quarters – Three coin max bet and $100,000 reset.
Dollars – Two coin max bet and $250,000 reset.

The highest payout so far occurred on a quarter machine

in Missouri, in the amount of almost $2 million. The jackpot is paid immediately on both the quarter and dollar versions.

Millionaire 777s

Right now, this Bally WAPS can only be found in Nevada, but it is so popular that by the time this book is published, it will surely have spread to other jurisdictions. These are dollar machines with a reset of $1 million.

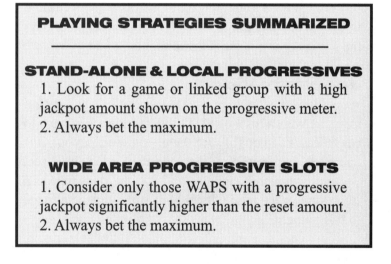

PLAYING STRATEGIES SUMMARIZED

STAND-ALONE & LOCAL PROGRESSIVES
1. Look for a game or linked group with a high jackpot amount shown on the progressive meter.
2. Always bet the maximum.

WIDE AREA PROGRESSIVE SLOTS
1. Consider only those WAPS with a progressive jackpot significantly higher than the reset amount.
2. Always bet the maximum.

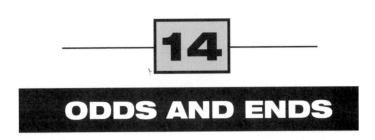

14

ODDS AND ENDS

Just when we think we have covered the entire subject of slot machines, there are still a few odds and ends left over that don't seem to fit in any of the previous chapters. Yet, they are important enough that they should be included, starting with Misconceptions. The other odds and ends are Slot Tournaments, Antique Slot Machines, and an unpleasant but important discussion about the IRS.

12 SLOT MACHINE MISCONCEPTIONS

During the hundred-odd years that slot machines have existed, many myths and fallacies have built up around them. If you have been reading this book with reasonable care, you will not be misled by the many stories and rumors that circulate among avid slot players. Nevertheless, to keep you from straying down that delusional path of old wives tales, we will try to debunk the most persistent of the slot legends.

1. When jackpot symbols start appearing just above or below the payline, the machine is ready to hit a big one.

False. Slot machines were originally designed so that you could only see the symbols that fell right on the payline. The fact that you can see above and below the payline is a deliberate design feature. It invites you to wonder what might have been and is called wishful thinking. This is part of the overall psychology used by casinos to encourage you to keep playing.

2. You are more likely to win if you pull the handle instead of pressing the MAX BET or SPIN buttons.

> **False.** In modern slot machines, when there is a handle, it is connected to an electrical switch that activates the same circuit as the switches under the MAX BET and SPIN buttons. In other words, the electrical circuits in the machine don't know whether you pulled the handle or pushed a button. Pull handles are fast disappearing, so this will soon become a moot point.

3. The loosest slot machines are located near the entrance and on the main aisles.

> **False.** This is a long-held belief among slot players, so those machines are usually pretty busy. The slot managers also know this myth, so many of them put tighter machines in those locations, knowing they will get played anyway. To learn where the loosest machines are located, read the section on Finding the Loosest Slots in Chapter 7.

4. If someone hits a jackpot at a machine you just left, that would have been your jackpot if you had stayed with it.

False. All modern slot machines contain a random number generator (RNG) that controls the outcome of each spin. While the machine is idle, the RNG spawns thousands of numbers every second until someone hits the SPIN or MAX BET button. Consequently, if the person who sat down at the game you just left hesitated a split second before spinning the reels, she probably would not have won that jackpot.

5. After a machine pays a big jackpot, it will run tighter for a while to make up for the loss.

False. The RNG (see above) does not have a memory. It just keeps on spitting out random numbers as though nothing had happened. In fact, it is theoretically and statistically possible for a machine to hit a big jackpot twice in a row.

6. Casinos can flip a switch to reset the slot machines to pay better (or worse) on weekends (or nights).

False. There is no switch. To modify the payback of a machine (making it looser or tighter) would require changing a chip in the machine's microprocessor. To legally do this requires prior approval from the gaming commission, and the actual modification usually has to be performed by a factory mechanic while being observed by an agent of the gaming commission.

7. When someone hits a jackpot, a slot mechanic often opens the machine and resets the payback percentage to a lower value.

> **False.** Modifying the payback is not a simple procedure. See above.

8. If an attendant or mechanic opens your machine for any reason, it will stop paying off.

> **False.** The slot mechanic is your friend; his job is to make sure the machine is operating properly. He cannot affect the payoffs in any way. Neither can the attendant who clears a coin jam or refills the coin hopper.

9. A slot machine will pay off less (or more) if you insert the casino's slot club card.

> **False.** The slot club card reader has no effect on the operation of the machine. Don't deprive yourself of this major benefit that can get you valuable comps and even cash rebates.

10. If you use a slot club card, the casino will report your winnings to the IRS.

> **False.** The legal requirement is that the casino must report single wins of $1200 or greater, and they will do this whether or not you have been using a slot club card. The casino does not add up smaller wins and report them—why should they if they don't legally have to?

11. A machine will pay better (or worse) if you insert paper currency rather than coins.

> **False.** The RNG determines the outcome of the next spin, and it does not know whether you inserted a bill, dropped in a coin, or played a credit. Nor should it care. Nor should the casino care.

12. A slot machine will pay better if you use cold (or hot) coins.

> **False.** This is a very old myth, and it is so silly that it doesn't deserve a response. However, it keeps recurring and doesn't want to die. Be aware that there are no temperature sensors in the coin mechanism (why should there be?), so the machine doesn't know if the coins you are inserting are hot or cold. In fact, the RNG doesn't even know whether you inserted a coin, a bill, or played a credit (see above).

SLOT TOURNAMENTS

We know that there are poker tournaments and that there are blackjack tournaments, and we also know that the most skillful players usually win. But what in the world is a slot tournament? What skill do slot machine players apply to win such a tournament? The fact is, the only skill needed in a slot tournament is the ability to hit the SPIN button as rapidly as possible. The more reel spins that can be achieved in the allotted time period, the more winning points or credits are likely to be achieved.

Actually, most slot tournaments are nothing more than casino promotions. As such, they are usually a good deal for the contestants, especially the 100-percent equity tournaments, where all the entry fee funds are returned to the contestants in the form of prizes. Although the rules vary from casino to casino, prizes are often awarded to the top ten winners, along with a booby prize. Additionally, casinos often give the players free buffets, T-shirts, and other goodies.

If you are interested in tournament play, be sure to join the slot clubs of your favorite casinos. They will then notify you of future tournaments and how to sign up. When you are trying to decide where to play, look for a cashless tournament with 100% equity. Cashless means that your only monetary risk is the entry fee—the actual slot play costs you nothing.

Of course, when casinos do anything that seems to be a bargain, they eventually expect a payoff. By bringing all these slot players together, they hope that the contestants will be practicing on the other slots in the casino when they are not playing in the tournament. In fact, it can be so lucrative for a casino, that some of them even offer free tournaments to their active slot club members. This is just another good reason to join the slot clubs.

BUYING ANTIQUE SLOT MACHINES

If you are a real slot machine devotee and miss the action when you are at home, you can purchase your own machine and play to your heart's content. A slot machine is a neat addition to a rumpus or game room. In most states you may legally own an antique slot machine, so long as you don't use it for commercial purposes. If you have the storage space, you may also be interested in collecting antique machines. This can be a profitable hobby, since most of them will increase in value over time.

Before you make a sizeable investment, however, it would be prudent to obtain at least one book on the subject. A good start is the *Slot Machine Buyer's Handbook* by David Saul, which is available from standard on-line sources such as Amazon.com.

Before buying your first machine, you should consult the following list to see what the legal rules are for your state. Since these statutes are occasionally modified, you should also check with your state attorney general's office for the latest rulings.

ALABAMA	All slot machines prohibited.
ALASKA	All slot machines are legal.
ARIZONA	All slot machines are legal.
ARKANSAS	All slot machines are legal.
CALIFORNIA	Must be at least 25 years old.
COLORADO	Pre-1984 slot machines only.
CONNECTICUT	All slot machines prohibited.
DELAWARE	Must be at least 25 years old.
DIST. COLUMBIA	Pre-1952 slot machines only.
FLORIDA	Must be at least 20 years old.
GEORGIA	Pre-1950 slot machines only.
HAWAII	All slot machines prohibited.
IDAHO	Pre-1950 slot machines only.
ILLINOIS	Must be at least 25 years old.
INDIANA	All slot machines prohibited.
IOWA	Must be at least 25 years old.
KANSAS	Pre-1950 slot machines only.
KENTUCKY	All slot machines are legal.

LOUISIANA	Must be at least 25 years old.
MAINE	All slot machines are legal.
MARYLAND	Must be at least 25 years old.
MASSACHUSETTS	Must be at least 30 years old.
MICHIGAN	Must be at least 25 years old.
MINNESOTA	All slot machines are legal.
MISSISSIPPI	Must be at least 25 years old.
MISSOURI	Must be at least 30 years old.
MONTANA	Must be at least 25 years old.
NEBRASKA	All slot machines prohibited.
NEVADA	All slot machines are legal.
NEW HAMPSHIRE	Must be at least 25 years old.
NEW JERSEY	Must be at least 30 years old.

NEW MEXICO   Although statute says slot machines at least 25 years old are legal, attorney general ruled in 2000 that only a licensed dealer can buy or sell them.

NEW YORK	Must be at least 30 years old.
NORTH CAROLINA	Must be at least 25 years old.
NORTH DAKOTA	Must be at least 25 years old.
OHIO	All slot machines are legal.
OKLAHOMA	Must be at least 25 years old.
OREGON	Must be at least 25 years old.
PENNSYLVANIA	Pre-1941 slot machines only.
RHODE ISLAND	All slot machines are legal.
SOUTH CAROLINA	All slot machines prohibited.
SOUTH DAKOTA	Must be at least 25 years old.
TENNESSEE	All slot machines prohibited.
TEXAS	All slot machines are legal.
UTAH	All slot machines are legal.
VERMONT	Pre-1954 slot machines only.
VIRGINIA	All slot machines are legal.
WASHINGTON	Must be at least 25 years old.
WEST VIRGINIA	All slot machines are legal.
WISCONSIN	All slot machines prohibited.
WYOMING	Must be at least 25 years old.

In most states where slot machine ownership is legal, it is with the proviso that the machine may not be used for gambling. The ages and years in the above list refer to the date of manufacture, except in Colorado where it refers to the date the machine was introduced.

Most dealers of used and antique slot machines will know the exact age of the machines they sell, and they should also know the latest statutes and rulings for all the states. When you purchase a machine, be sure to get a certification from the seller that clearly states the year of manufacture.

ABOUT THE IRS

The relationship between gambling and the IRS is a complex subject that even confounds lawyers and accountants specializing in this area. In this section, we are not giving you any specific tax or legal advice, but only making you aware of certain IRS requirements. It is valuable to know about some of these things before encountering them in a real situation.

If you engage in casino transactions of more than $10,000, you should consult an accountant familiar with gaming laws. Casinos must report all cash transactions in excess of $10,000 to the IRS. They must also report an aggregate of cash transactions that occur within a 24-hour period and total more than $10,000.

If you place a large bet at a sports book, cash-in chips, or even cash a check larger than $10,000, it must be reported. This is just a reporting requirement (presumably to control money laundering) and doesn't mean you have to pay taxes on the transaction. The state of Nevada also has a similar reporting requirement.

The IRS rule that is most important to slot players is the requirement for the casino to report any slot machine jackpot of $1200 or more by submitting a W-2G form. If you won your jackpot during a slot tournament, however, the IRS reporting requirement drops to $600.

Such winnings are considered ordinary income by the IRS and must be reported under "Other Income" on your 1040 tax return. Be sure you attach a copy of the W-2G to your return, or you will eventually get a letter from the IRS asking where it is.

You can reduce the tax burden (up to the amount of your winnings) if you can prove that you had offsetting gambling losses in the same year. Such losses cannot be subtracted from itemized winnings, but must be listed separately on Schedule A under "Miscellaneous Deductions." However, if your itemized deductions don't exceed the standard deduction, your gambling losses will not be useful as an offset. Also, keep in mind that you cannot reduce your overall tax by taking a *net* gambling loss— you can only offset winnings.

How do you prove that you had gambling losses? By keeping a detailed dairy of all your gambling activities. How detailed? The IRS recommendation is that you record the date, the time, the amount of your wins and losses, the type of game, its denomination, and the serial number of each machine played.

You should also record the name and location of the casino, and the names of any people (witnesses) with you at the time. Supporting documentation such as airline ticket receipts and hotel bills will help to convince an IRS auditor that you were actually there.

However, unless you are a professional in the business of gambling *and* your trip was primarily for business purposes, do not try to deduct expenses such as transportation, hotel rooms, or restaurants.

Once you get used to the idea, you will see that keeping a diary is not as daunting as it first appears. How you actually deal with it, that is, what you put in and what you leave out, is entirely your decision. Just keep in mind that if the entire diary does not appear to be reasonable, an auditor may judge that it is inaccurate and disallow it.

Regardless of the above advice, you don't bother to keep a record because, like most people, you're there for just a few days and don't expect to hit a big jackpot. You are smart enough, however, to join the slot club in the hope that you will get a comp or two. It doesn't surprise you that after three days of playing the slots, you are down $1500. The fourth day you hit a $2000 jackpot, and you are elated until the casino hands you a W-2G form. It is then that you realize you will have to pay taxes on the entire $2000, even though you had already lost $1500.

"What a bummer!" you complain. "I lose money and have to pay taxes, anyway!" A floor manager hears your griping and advises you to go to the slot club counter and get a record of your slot play. Sure enough, the record shows proof of your losses over the previous three days so that you can offset most of the jackpot winnings. Moral: Be sure to join the slot club—besides the normal club benefits, it can save you a bundle on taxes.

GLOSSARY

Action — The total amount of money bet. Win or lose, the same dollar bet fifty times, constitutes $50 worth of action.

Banking game — A slot machine in which points or some form of assets are accumulated in a "bank" and eventually paid out as credits.

Bankroll — The amount of money a person designates for gambling.

Bar — A common symbol on slot machine reels.

BET MAX button — Pressing this button causes two actions to occur. First, it registers a maximum credit bet, whatever it might be for that machine. If it is a two-coin machine it will register two coins, if it is a three-coin machine it will register three coins, and so forth. Second, it automatically spins the reels; you don't have to press the SPIN button. On some machines, this button is marked PLAY MAX CREDITS.

BET ONE button — Pressing this button will register in the machine as a one-credit bet. It is exactly the same as if you put one coin into the slot, which is an alternative. If you press the button a second time, it will register as a two-credit bet, and so forth. On some machines, this button is marked BET 1 CREDIT.

Big bertha — A giant slot machine with eight to ten reels, often placed near the entrance of a casino to lure potential slot players. Not a good machine to play.

Blank — A stop on a slot machine reel with no symbols. A few machines give a minimum payout for three blanks.

Bonus game — A slot machine in which certain symbol combinations cause a bonus mode to appear on a secondary screen.

Buy-a-pay game — Another term for an option-buy game.

Buy-your-pay game — Another term for an option-buy game.

Cage — Short for cashier's cage, where casino chips may be exchanged for cash and other financial transactions may be consummated.

Candle — The light on top of a slot cabinet that indicates the machine denomination and signals for an attendant when you press the CHANGE button.

Carousel — A group of slot machines, usually surrounding an elevated change booth.

CASH OUT button — Pressing this button converts any credits accumulated in the machine to coins. This button is sometimes marked CASH/CREDIT or COLLECT.

Cash ticket — A printed paper coupon that can be redeemed for cash or inserted in another ticket-equipped game machine.

Casino advantage — The mathematical edge a casino has over the player, which is usually stated as a percentage.

Casino host — The casino employee who caters to the needs of high-stakes players.

Casino manager — The head honcho for all gaming operations.

GLOSSARY

Change booth — A booth set up to convert a player's currency to coins or coins to currency.

CHANGE button — Pressing this button summons the change person. You should also press the button whenever something seems to go wrong with the machine. This button is often marked SERVICE.

Change person — The casino employee who roams the slot machine area and makes change for the players.

Chasing losses — Raising the betting level in an attempt to recoup losses. Not a recommended procedure.

Cherry — A common symbol on slot machine reels.

Cold machine — A slot machine that is paying less than its expected payback.

Comp — Shortened term for the *complimentary* rewards, such as rooms, meals, or show tickets, given to big players.

Credits — Instead of paying out coins, most modern slot machines keep track of winnings in the form of credits that can be converted to coins by pressing the CASH OUT button. The accumulated credits can also be played.

Denomination — The minimum coin or credit value required to play a slot machine. The most popular denominations are nickel, quarter, and dollar.

Edge — The mathematical advantage in a game.

Even money — A bet that, if won, pays one-to-one odds.

Glass — The posted chart on a slot machine showing the winning symbol combinations and the payouts.

Handpay — A jackpot payoff that is made by an attendant rather than by the machine.

High roller — A gambler who plays for high stakes.

Hopper — The container inside a slot machine that holds the coins used to pay off wins or a cashout.

Hot machine — A slot machine that is paying more than its expected payback.

House edge — The difference between the actual odds and the payoff odds, usually stated as a percentage. It is the mathematical advantage a casino has over the player.

House percentage — The difference between the amount of money taken in by a machine and the amount paid out over the long term. This difference is the casino profit.

Jackpot — The largest payout on any particular machine. Also, any big win with a large payout.

Lemon — A common symbol on slot machine reels.

Line — Short for payline.

Line game — Another term for a multiple payline game.

Local progressive — Similar progressive machines, usually in a bank or carousel, that are linked together within a single casino.

Loose machine — A slot machine programmed for a higher than average long-term payback.

Multi-Game machine — A slot machine in which the player has a choice of several different games, usually including video poker.

GLOSSARY

Multiple payline game — A slot machine that has more than one payline. Wagering more coins or credits can activate the additional paylines.

Multiplier game — A slot machine in which the number of coins or credits wagered multiplies the amount of the payout.

Odds — The mathematical ratio of the number of ways to win versus the number of ways to lose.

One-armed bandit — An old slang term used for slot machines, indicating that the payouts were very poor.

Option-buy game — A slot machine in which additional winning symbol combinations are activated by betting the maximum number of coins or credits.

Payback — The total long-term winnings as a percent of the total amount bet.

Payline — A line across the window in front of the reels that shows where a winning symbol combination has to be aligned for a payoff. Some games have several paylines.

Payoff — The amount paid for a winning symbol combination.

Payout — Another term for payoff.

Paytable — A chart, usually above the reels, showing the winning symbol combinations and the payout amounts. On a video machine, the paytable may be displayed on the screen by pressing the PAYTABLE button.

PAYTABLE button — Pressing this button on a video game brings the paytable to the screen. Often, it is several pages in length. Sometimes this button is marked SEE PAYS.

Progressive jackpot — A dynamic top jackpot that grows larger by pooling a fraction of each wager as the games are played. Groups of machines are usually linked together, all contributing to the same progressive jackpot.

Random number generator (RNG) — The RNG is one of the chips on the internal computer board of a slot machine. It generates thousands of random numbers a second, and each random number sequence defines a specific set of reel symbols.

Reel — Side-by-side rotating wheels displaying various symbols on the outside rims. A small section of the reels may be viewed through a window, which usually exposes about three rows of symbols.

Scatter symbols — Symbols that result in a payoff when they appear anywhere in the reel window.

Secondary screen — A bonus screen that is initiated by certain symbol combinations.

Shift boss — The top manager during the course of a single work shift.

Slot floor — The area of a casino designated for slot machines.

Slot manager — The top manager for the slot department of the casino.

Slot mechanic — The casino employee who is responsible for maintaining the proper mechanical and electronic operation of the slot machines.

SPIN button — After indicating the number of credits or inserting one or more coins, pressing this button starts the game by causing the reels to spin. On some machines, this button is marked SPIN REELS.

GLOSSARY

Spinning reel machine — A slot machine with mechanical spinning reels, although the reels are now computer controlled.

Stake — Another term for bankroll.

Stand-alone progressive — A solitary progressive slot machine that is not linked to any other machine.

Stop — The position of a reel when it comes to rest. A reel may stop when a symbol is under the payline or when the blank space between two symbols falls under the payline.

Substitute symbol — Another term for wild symbol.

Symbols — The pictures of various objects that appear on the slot machine reels.

Tight machine — A slot machine programmed for a lower than average long-term payback.

Top box — An illuminated case above the reels or video screen that displays the game theme and/or additional features.

Touchscreen — A video screen where you can touch an object to select it.

Video machine — A slot machine in which the spinning reels are simulated on a video screen.

Wide Area Progressive Slot (WAPS) — One of a large number of similar progressive machines that are linked together over a wide geographic area such as a city or a state.

Wild symbol — A symbol that can substitute for any other symbol on the reels to produce a winning combination. Often called *substitute symbols*.

Window — The glass area in front of the reels where the payline and the symbols are viewed.

GRI'S PROFESSIONAL VIDEO POKER STRATEGY
Win Money at Video Poker! With the Odds!

For the **first time,** and for **serious players only**, the GRI **Professional Video Poker** strategy is released so you too can play to win! **You read it right** - this strategy gives you the **mathematical advantage** over the casino and what's more, it's **easy to learn!**

PROFESSIONAL STRATEGY SHOWS YOU HOW TO WIN WITH THE ODDS - This **powerhouse strategy,** played for **big profits** by an **exclusive** circle of **professionals,** people who make their living at the machines, is now made available to you! You too can win - with the odds - and this **winning strategy** shows you how!

HOW TO PLAY FOR A PROFIT - You'll learn the **key factors** to play on a **pro level**: which machines will turn you a profit, break-even and win rates, hands per hour and average win per hour charts, time value, team play and more! You'll also learn big play strategy, alternate jackpot play, high and low jackpot play and key strategies to follow.

WINNING STRATEGIES FOR ALL MACHINES - This **comprehensive, advanced pro package** not only shows you how to win money at the 8-5 progressives, but also, the **winning strategies** for 10s or better, deuces wild, joker's wild, flat-top, progressive and special options features.

BE A WINNER IN JUST ONE DAY - In just one day, after learning our strategy, you will have the skills to **consistently win money** at video poker - with the odds. The strategies are easy to use under practical casino conditions.

FREE BONUS - PROFESSIONAL PROFIT EXPECTANCY FORMULA ($15 VALUE) - For serious players, we're including this free bonus essay which explains the professional profit expectancy principles of video poker and how to relate them to real dollars and cents in your game.

To order send just $50 by check or money order to:
Cardoza Publishing, P.O. Box 1500, Cooper Station, New York, NY 10276

144